11.49

Karen Commings

Manx Cats

Everything about
Purchase, Care,
Nutrition, Grooming,
and Behavior

Filled with Full-color Photographs
Illustrations by Michele Earle-Bridges

BARRON'S

2 CONTENTS

INTRODUCTION TO THE MANX

An Unfinished Symphony

When one first sets eyes on the tailless cat known as the Manx, one can't help but feel that something is missing—as if Mother Nature, having grown tired before her task was done, left her tiny creation incomplete and never came back to finish the job. Like an unfinished symphony, the Manx cat is compelled to enrich our lives with a song for which the last verse will remain forever unwritten. Although to some, the lack of a tail may seem curious at first, the Manx's missing appendage in no way diminishes its stature as a bona fide member of the cat kingdom or the cat fancy. The Manx cat is an affectionate and devoted animal whose sweet expression and round body make it as captivating and lovable as a teddy bear and whose sturdy appearance and handsome good looks are admired by cat lovers and cat fanciers everywhere.

Short-tailed cats can be found all over the world, but the only one that is bred to be completely without a tail is the Manx. Unlike the Japanese and the American Bobtails, two breeds whose genetic makeup affects only the length of the tail, the Manx is the result of a natural mutation—a mistake of nature that alters one or more of the nucleotides in a piece of DNA, the genetic composition of which restricts the length of the cat's spinal column. The result is complete taillessness or tails with lengths in between total absence of a tail and one that is full length. It isn't only the lack of a tail that makes a Manx. The breed's hind legs are markedly longer than the front legs, making the Manx's rump higher than its shoulders.

The Manx has a sturdy, compact bone structure and cobby body—short in length, broad in the beam, and low on the legs. The back forms a continuous arch to the tail area. The overall impression of the Manx is one of roundness: round body, round head, round cheeks and round eyes. The facial features impart a wide-eyed, innocent expression to what is already a lovable cat. The Manx's short, dense double coat comes in every color, including the pointed colors typical of the Siamese and Himalayan breeds. The pointed colors are not accepted in every pedigreed cat registry, however.

The Missing Links

The Manx gene for taillessness is an *incomplete dominant* gene. It will show up even if only one parent carries it. *Incomplete dominance* means the heterozygote exhibits the

The Manx, although known for its taillessness, has several tail lengths: from front, rumpy, rumpy riser, stumpy, and longy.

define exactly what a tail is. A tail is more than just an appendage attached to the hindquarters of any animal that is supposed to have one; anatomically speaking, it is the extension of an animal's spinal column. Moving from top to bottom, the cat's spine consists of 7 cervical (neck), 13 thoracic (upper back), 7 lumbar (lower back), 3 sacral (pelvic) and between 19 and 21 coccygeal, or caudal (tail), vertebrae, which are numbered from the top down. There is no fixed number of coccygeal vertebrae in a cat; it varies from breed to breed. Breeds that have shorter tails, such as Persians, American Shorthairs, Exotic Shorthairs, and Scottish Folds, have fewer coccygeal vertebrae than those with longer, whippy tails, such as Siamese, Oriental Shorthairs, and Abyssinians. Thus the last lumbar vertebrae is numbered L7, and it attaches to S1 (sacral one). Sacral three (S3) attaches to the first caudal vertebra (Ca1). The Manx spine from the skull to the sacrum is perfectly normal. The three sacral vertebrae are present and fused to support the hips. The Manx spine, considered shorter than that of other breeds such as the Maine Coon Cat, is shorter because each individual vertebra is shorter and because the extension—the tail—is missing most or all its parts.

effects of both members of a pair of genes, called *alleles*. Unlike other purebred cats in which the genetic makeup that causes a breed-specific trait is called homozygous (both genes in a pair for the trait match), the Manx is heterozygous, which means it possesses one gene for taillessness and one for a tail. Where there is a copy of the dominant tailless allele in the gene pair, there may be various lengths other than full length of the tail in the phenotype (the observable appearance of the cat). As a result, there is a probability that cats with different tail lengths will be born in any given litter of Manx kittens. Fetuses that inherit the tailless gene from *both* parents fail to develop.

A Cat Tail

Before describing the lengths in which the Manx tail can be found, it is useful to first

Rumpies, Stumpies, and Rumpy Risers

On all cats, including the Manx, the last two or three tail vertebrae are tapered. This is noticeable to anyone placing a hand around a cat's tail and sliding it from the top to the tip. Even in tailless Manx cats, one or two of the tapered vertebrae are still present, which means that the missing ones are the lower-numbered ones closer to the cat's sacrum. A tail-lesss Manx is called a rumpy and is prized among breeders and cat fanciers.

The Manx with a tail that consists of up to three coccygeal vertebrae is called a rumpy riser. Manx cats with short, stubby tails that have varying numbers of vertebrae present are called stumpies, and those with full tails are called longies. Only rumpy and rumpy riser Manx cats are eligible for championship status in the show ring, although the rumpy riser tail with fixed vertebrae so that it stops the judge's hand as it sweeps down and over the cat's back is penalized. In the Cat Fanciers' Association (CFA), the world's largest registry of pedigreed cats, stumpies and longies are allowed to be exhibited only in the any other variety (AOV) class. Although stumpies and longies are not eligible for championship competition, they are valued in breeding if their type—the arrangement of the overall parts of the cat in accordance with breed specifications—is good, because they add sturdiness to the pedigree line. Even longy-to-longy Manx breeding will produce rumpy and stumpy kittens.

The Long and Short of It

In addition to various tail lengths, the Manx cat comes in two different coat lengths—the shorthaired version and a medium-length, longhaired version. The gene for long hair in

Shorthaired (top) and longhaired Manx

a cat is a recessive gene so that both parents must have the gene present for them to pro-duce longhaired kittens. Because the longhair gene is recessive, there is only a one in four chance of longhair kittens in a litter that is produced by shorthaired cats carrying the longhair gene.

Like its shorthaired counterpart, the long-haired Manx can have a tail of any length. Its body type is the same as the shorthaired Manx and must conform to the breed standard in every way but in the length of its hair. The longhaired Manx has a double coat with thick awn hairs and longer guard hairs, resulting in a coat that is dense and silky. The coat gradually lengthens from the cat's shoulders to its rump. The breeches, lower belly, and neck ruff are longer than the hair on the rest of its body.

Although longhaired Manx cats probably have been around as long as the shorthaired ones, written history documenting the longhaired version is relatively short. In the 1960s, a pair of Canadian pedigreed, shorthaired Manx cats produced several longhaired kittens, which in turn were bred to generate additional long-haired offspring. Longhaired Manx appeared in American Cat Association shows as early as 1963.

Support for separate breed classification of the longhaired Manx came early from north of the border when the Canadian Cat Association (CCA), the pedigreed cat registry in Canada, recognized it for championship status. Called a Cymric (pronounced kim-rick), the Welsh word for Welsh, the name for the longhaired Manx came from a Canadian breeder whose Welsh grandmother coined the term because she had seen many longhaired tailless cats in Wales. In 1976, the International United Cymric Association was formed to muster support of the longhaired Manx. In 1989, CFA voted to allow the longhaired Manx championship status. It is shown as a Manx but in a separate division. In other registries, the Cymric is a separate breed.

History of the Manx Breed

Although the exact origin of the Manx cat is unknown, most cat fanciers attribute its existence to a natural mutation that occurred hundreds of years ago within the feral cat population on the 227-square-mile (588-km) Isle of Man, which is in the middle of the Irish Sea, midway between Liverpool, England, and Belfast, Ireland.

Romans, Vikings, Scots, and Cats

The Isle of Man has a long history dating from the time of the Roman emperor, Caesar, who named it Mona. In the first century A.D.,

Pliny the elder, a Roman writer and encyclopedist, called the island Monapia. From the ninth to the thirteenth centuries, the Isle of Man was invaded and controlled by Vikings, a nordic people consisting of Danes, Swedes, and Norwegians whose trade routes extended to Europe, England, and beyond. Manx historian A.W. Moore describes the fabled first king of the Isle, Mannanan, who gave the Isle the name of Manavia Insula. Following the Vikings were the Scots and English who traded control of the Isle of Man for the next 200 years. Both the names Man and Mann are used in island records from the fifteenth to the seventeenth centuries. Historically, the language spoken on the Isle was a form of Celtic, but today English is the common tongue. The word Manx applies to the cats and the residents of the Isle. In this book, Manx will refer only to the breed of cat. Today, the Isle of Man is an internally self governing dependent territory of the British Crown, but is not part of the United Kingdom. Tynwald, the island's 1,000-year-old Parliament, makes its own laws and oversees all internal administration, fiscal, and social policies. External issues, such as foreign representation and defense, are administered on the island's behalf by the United Kingdom.

The Viking and the Pussycat

Exactly how cats came to the Isle is unclear. The first cats could have arrived with the Romans whose conquests helped them spread throughout Europe the domestic cats they obtained as spoils of war when they conquered Egypt. Because of similarity in coat appearance between the longhaired Manx and the Norwegian Forest Cat, it has been hypothesized that the longhair gene was a result of the Isle's

Manx are affectionate and loyal, according to fanciers.

indigenous cats mating with longhaired cats arriving with the Viking invaders who, like many raiders and traders, kept cats on board as fur-covered mousetraps to keep the ships' stores from being consumed by rodents. Another theory holds that, during the sixteenth century, merchant ships brought cats to the Isle of Man, where they bred isolated for centuries, during which time the spontaneous mutation that created the cat with no tail occurred. Veterinarian and breeder D.W. Kerruish, who ran the Manx-land cattery on the Isle of Man and wrote the 1964 book, *The Manx Cat,* believed that the Manx has its origins in the common shorthaired British cat that appeared in the British Isles 200 to 300 years ago. Dr. Kerruish points to the word stumpy, for which there is no word in the Manx language. He indicates that the word for stumpy in the Manx dictionary is an anglicized word indicating that the tailless cats on the Isle showed up there only after the English did. Although some scholars in the past speculated that tailless and short-tailed cats were taken to the Isle by Phoenician traders in ancient times, it is now known that the bobtailed cats of the Orient and the Manx are genetically different.

Whether the tailless gene was imported to the island or occurred spontaneously among the feral cat population already living there, the isolation of the Isle of Man was critical in the development of taillessness among the free-roaming cats populating its tiny land mass.

The existence of Manx cats has been documented for at least 200 years. Dr. Kerruish notes that the English landscape artist Joseph Turner had seven tailless cats as early as 1810, all of which came from the Isle of Man. Late in the nineteenth century, Isle of Man entrepreneurs bred Manx to be sold as souvenirs to eager tourists, with no thought given to the resulting type or condition of cat that was produced. As a result, many Manx cats and kittens were less than perfect specimens. Fishermen have transported Manx cats off the Isle to ports along their northern fishing routes. Today colonies of Manx cats are reputed to live on the Shetland Islands, a 552-square-mile (1,430-sq-km) group of 100 islands north of Scotland famous for their Shetland ponies and woollen garments. Like the Isle of Man, the Shetland Islands also fell under Viking rule for several centuries during their long history.

Manx Cattery

To prevent extinction of the Manx on the island, the government erected a cattery in Noble's Park in Douglas, the island's capital. Taken over by the Douglas Corporation in 1964, the cattery became a popular tourist attraction. The cattery closed in 1989, but the Manx cat population has remained steady. In addition to the handful of breeders of purebred Manx, many island residents breed unregistered Manx cats to help satisfy the demand for them on and off the island. In addition, there is a large feral cat population.

In 1997, the Mann Cat Sanctuary was established to provide a safe haven for rescued cats and kittens. Supported by donations, the sanctuary rehabilitates homeless cats, neuters them, and finds them new homes.

Manx cats with tails of all lengths were exhibited at London's Crystal Palace, the birthplace of the cat fancy, and in European cat shows in the latter part of the nineteenth and early part of the twentieth centuries. Although tails of all lengths were considered acceptable, the favored body type for competition was rounded and cobby. A Manx cat club was formed in Great Britain in 1901. King Edward VII, who succeeded his mother Queen Victoria to the British throne that same year, had Manx cats.

Manx cats became a part of the cat fancy in the United States. According to its oldest stud books, the CFA recognized the Manx as a breed in the 1920s. Although the taillessness is the result of a mutation, CFA considers Manx one of the "natural breeds," which means that both parents and all ancestors must be of the breed for the cat to be registered. Manx cats are enjoyed by cat lovers worldwide, and they are shown in every major pedigreed cat registry in the world.

Manx Personality

Like cats everywhere, each Manx is an individual with its own personality, unique in the way that it views the world and responds to it. As soon as one points to a common characteristic of the breed, a Manx breeder or owner holds up a cat that does not even come close to having the representative quality that many think separates the Manx from other breeds. Because a reputable breeder will have spent time socializing his or her kittens before placing them in good homes, inquire about the personality of the individual kitten that strikes your fancy when you visit the breeder. Kitten personalities develop when they get into their own domain, however, so that shy, reserved Manx kitten that you found so appealing at the cattery may become the boss of your household once it has acclimated to living with you.

In spite of their individuality, most Manx share many qualities that make them appealing to cat lovers and prospective buyers. Manx breeders describe the cats as affectionate, outgoing, and loyal companions. Although they may form a special bond with one member of a family, they are demonstrative with all people in the household, including children who have been taught to handle them gently and with care. In spite of their social nature, not all Manx will greet strangers readily. If you entertain regularly, chances are your Manx will become accustomed to friends who come to call and will enjoy them as much as you do. If guests are a rarity, your Manx may choose to sit back and observe before deciding to participate in the activities. If you have a rodent problem in your home, expect your Manx's natural hunting ability to turn your house into a mouse-free zone.

Because of their rounded appearance, gentleness and loving nature, it's easy to want to cuddle with your Manx kitten or cat, and you will find your Manx ready and eager to oblige. Because of its easygoing nature and loving disposition, your Manx may follow you from room to

Tall Tales

Because the Manx's origins are shrouded in mystery, many legends have arisen about how it lost its tail. One myth attributes the Manx taillessness to the Vikings, who, when they invaded the Isle of Man, attempted to slice off the native cats' tails to adorn their helmets. Fearful for their kittens, mother cats bit off the tails of their offspring to prevent the tails from becoming furry frills. Another myth attributes the Manx to a cross between a cat and a rabbit in an attempt to explain not only the lack of a tail but also the hopping gait found in some poorly bred Manx.

A favorite fable puts cats on the Ark in the time of the great flood. The pair of cats were the last of the animals to board the Ark because their common sense and foresight would not allow them to enter without taking a mouse along for food. After Noah had herded all the other animals safely inside, the rain began to fall. Noah grew impatient and fearful at leaving the ark door open for the cats. At the last minute, the cats squeezed through the door as Noah slammed it shut, cutting off their tails.

In the 1903 *The Book of the Cat*, author Frances Simpson recounts a folk tale from the Isle of Man that tells the Manx people's version of Noah and how the Manx lost its tail.

Noah, sailing o'er the seas
Ran fast aground on Ararat;
His dog then made a spring and took
The tail from off a pretty cat.
Puss through the window quick did fly,
And bravely through the waters swam
Nor ever stopped till high and dry,
She landed on the Calf of Man.
Thus tailless Puss earned Mona's thanks
And ever after was called Manx.

Another tale attributes the origins of the Manx to the Spaniards who brought them aboard the Spanish Armada, a fleet of ships dispatched in 1588 by King Phillip II of Spain, who sought to invade England. One of the ships of the Spanish Armada was fabled to have run aground near the Isle, forcing its hapless feline and human occupants to swim ashore in the cold Atlantic waters. History, however, records no such event and, as with all tall tales, we are left to discover the truth about the origins of the Manx wherever we can find it.

room and participate in whatever you are doing, whether you're reading a newspaper or working at the computer. Your Manx will gladly sit in your lap as you watch television or keep you company in bed at night. In fact, one Manx breeder easily placed his kittens with the advertising slogan, "Unemployed cat seeks position as bed warmer."

A Manx can be expected to live as long as any other breed or type of cat—an average of 14 years—so you and your Manx will share many years together. When you've selected a Manx, you have chosen a close companion. A Manx kitten will be your best playmate; a Manx adult will be your best friend.

FINDING YOUR PUREBRED MANX

Decisions, Decisions...

Before plunging headfirst into Manx ownership, the first question to ask yourself is, "Why do I want a cat?" Holding a cat and listening to it purr has been shown to reduce stress and lower blood pressure. Because cats engage in all kinds of interesting and amusing activities, cat-watching is a favorite pastime among cat owners. But the other side of the coin is that cats require time, energy, and attention from their people as well as a considerable amount of money for food, supplies, and veterinary care.

Cats kept indoors live an average of 14 years or more these days, thanks to advances in feline medicine and nutrition. The Manx is a sturdy, healthy breed. Given proper care, your Manx will spend many years with you and your family.

Purchasing a pedigreed cat requires a commitment to its care throughout its life. What will happen to your Manx if you move? What will happen to your Manx if you have a baby? If you adopt a dog or other pet? If your Manx develops a health or behavior problem? Before adding a Manx to your household, make sure your home life is stable, and your Manx will be a continued part of it. Once you are certain that you can provide good care for a Manx throughout its entire life, you will be embarking on one of the greatest joys and pleasures known to man—living with a cat companion.

Before purchasing your Manx, spend some time thinking about what kind of Manx you want. Be prepared, however, to have the perfect kitten or cat just leap out at you when you meet it, despite all your analysis. The perfect cat, like the perfect mate, is sometimes just a matter of chemistry.

Kitten or Adult Cat

Everyone loves kittens. They are playful, energetic, and fun to watch. If you adopt a kitten, be prepared to provide plenty of outlets for their highly charged energy. Many prospective buyers assume that kittens are more easily taught and trained than are adults. Kittens are often looked upon as able to bond with their new owners and acclimate to their new homes more easily than an older cat.

Manx breeders usually let their kittens go to new homes when they are 14 to 16 weeks old. This gives the breeder an opportunity to evaluate the kitten's potential as a show cat. The breeder will be able to determine which kittens should be sold as pets and which as show cats, if they are not going to be added to the seller's own breeding program.

Kittens depend on their mothers not just as a food supply, but also for the natural antibodies that help them build up their immune systems. Once they are weaned, they depend on their human owners to help the immune process along by giving them vaccinations to prevent certain diseases. By the time a kitten is 3.5 months old, it should have had two series of kitten vaccinations, which the seller should provide. Many breeders alter their pet quality cats before sale, and, although altering can occur at an early age, the surgery is typically not performed before the animal is three months old.

Purchasing an older kitten has advantages, too. You will be better able to evaluate the kitten's health when it is three to four months old. Some problems, such as bowel and bladder conditions, will not show up until after weaning. Diarrhea, which is common among kittens, usually clears up once the kitten is weaned and on solid food. A kitten's mother will teach it many of the skills it will need to cope with life. Some breeders feel that allowing kittens to have the adult supervision of their mothers for three to four months makes them better able to adjust and adapt to a new home when they are bought. Expect your three- to four-month-old kitten to be litter trained.

Adopting a Manx

If a more sedate feline companion appeals to you, consider adopting an adult Manx. Many breeders sell adult cats that are no longer part of a breeding program or no longer take part in the show circuit. These older cats can be wonderful, loving companions. Often the only cost for an adult Manx is the price of spay or neuter surgery, which the breeder will want to have performed before the sale. Altering can range from $20 for a male to $120 for a female, depending on where you live. If you are elderly, busy, or not very energetic, an adult Manx may be the perfect feline companion for you. Don't expect your adult Manx to be a couch potato, though. Cats, Manx included, retain their playfulness into adulthood.

Registering the Cat

As a buyer, you should not expect your kitten to be individually registered with the national association to which the breeder belongs. (See Exhibiting Your Manx page 81.) If you purchased your Manx from a reputable breeder, he or she will have registered the litter at the time of birth. The national association will return certificates for the individual kittens to the breeder to be passed along to the buyer at the time of purchase. Some breeders require proof of neutering before they will send the kitten's registration form to the buyer. You must return the certificate with the appropriate fees and your cat's name to the registry. If you have purchased an adult Manx, the cat will already be registered, and the breeder will give you the certificate at the time of purchase.

Manx kittens enjoy playing with a variety of toys.

Male or Female?

There are few differences between male and female Manx once they are neutered or spayed. Although some people prefer pets of one sex over the other, both make excellent, captivating companions. Male Manx cats reach 8 to 12 pounds and females range from 6 to 10 pounds. The Manx standard calls for a "medium sized cat," so expect your Manx not to be overly large or excessively small. Some breeders and cat owners think that male cats in general make better lapcats while females may be more circumspect. A lot of what may constitute differences between the sexes is dependent on the personality of the individual cat as well as its early experiences with humans so you are just as likely to find an adult female that wants to nap on your lap as you are a male.

If you are obtaining a Manx for breeding purposes, discuss with the seller obtaining an appropriate cat. Intact cats are more difficult to live with than those that are altered. Females come into heat periodically. The heat is accompanied by excessive yowling, posturing to potentially accept a male cat, even when none is in sight, and dribbling urine. Intact male cats will urine mark (spray) their living quarters to both attract a mate and let other males know that they are around.

Territorial and marking behaviors in which both sexes engage when they are intact are diminished or eliminated altogether once they are altered. Veterinarians perform spay and neuter surgery at early ages, but typically it occurs no later than 8 months for a male and 6 months for a female. If the female goes into heat before spaying, you may pay more for the surgery.

Hair Length

Except for some extra grooming that is required for a longhaired Manx, or Cymric, expect both types of Manx to be the same in terms of conformation to breed standard and personality. Your choice may be based on the time you have to allot to brushing and combing as well as personal preference for long or short hair.

Pet or Show Cat

Most pedigreed Manx kittens you will find for purchase are pet quality. Unfortunately, coupling the word "pet" with the word "quality" to describe those cats that are not good show candidates bestows a connotation that makes it seem as if kittens to which the term is applied are in some way substandard or defective. This couldn't be farther from the truth. The term *pet quality* may mean several things. It might imply that the cat in some way does not conform to breed standard. Perhaps the riser of the tail is too straight or the tail was docked. The trait, often invisible to the untrained eye, is something that will signify a Manx's lack of success in the show ring to a breeder, judge, or anyone experienced in the cat fancy. In some cases, it simply means that the cat was not chosen by the breeder to become part of the breeding stock or show circuit and is, therefore, sold as a pet kitten or cat even though its features make it a good show candidate. Breeders may choose a cat as a breeding female or male that may not necessarily be exhibited. Manx cats that don't adjust well emotionally to showing but that conform to standard (see page 85), have excellent pedigrees, and produce excellent kittens may become a part of the breeding program, although they may seldom see the show ring. In other cases, a breeder may sell a cat as

A Healthy Kitten or Cat

If you want to purchase a kitten, you will be better able to evaluate the kitten's health if you handle it first. The kitten should have a clean anal area with no bits of feces stuck to it. The kitten should not be sneezing, and no discharge should emanate from its eyes or nose. The kitten's coat should be healthy looking, not dull or shabby. There should be no bald patches or splotches of dry skin. As you gently fluff the kitten's hair, no black specks—the dried bits of flea feces and blood that are telltale signs of fleas—should fall out. The kitten's ears should be pink and clean inside. The kitten should be energetic and friendly, and, once it gets to know you, it should enjoy being held.

a pet simply because there are more homes for pet cats than there are for show or breeding cats.

If you want to exhibit your Manx, consider purchasing a show Manx. Before buying, learn the breed standard so you can evaluate your purchase. Visit cat shows and observe those Manx that are champions or grands. Learn what makes them different from other Manx. Talk to breeders and judges about the Manx and what makes a show cat.

Expect to pay more for a show cat than you would for a pet Manx. A show Manx may cost between $500 and $800 or more. A pet kitten costs about $300. A retired adult may cost up to $150. Although costs for purebred cats may seem high, they aren't when one considers the costs to the breeder of food, veterinary care, spay and neuter costs for a pet cat, and the time and effort that has been expended to socialize them and make them good companions. Add the costs that go into years of developing a line of well-bred Manx to see why conscientious breeders must ask the prices they do.

"Manx Syndrome"

Whenever a prospective Manx buyer begins to talk to friends, acquaintances, relatives, or co-workers about buying a Manx, it is not uncommon to hear cautionary statements that include phrases like "Manx syndrome" or "lethal gene" with little or no understanding about what the words mean. Surprisingly, some breeders of other pedigrees will emit statements such as, "Oh, Manx have so many health problems," or "They're such a fragile breed." Manx breeders the world over have described an anti-Manx bias among some veterinarians and even show judges, caused by perceptions having to do with taillessness and alleged health problems. If one listens to the casual

Before you buy a show cat, learn the breed standard so you can evaluate your purchase.

talk, it would seem as if every Manx cat has a built-in, self-destruct sequence that begins counting down at birth and ends a short time thereafter, causing harm to the cat and headaches and heartaches to its new owner. Not true. The phrase "Manx syndrome" has been used to describe a host of problems supposedly associated with the Manx gene. It was reported to include such difficulties as spine and rectal malformations, spina bifida, and, as reported in R. Robinson's, "Expressivity of the Manx Gene in Cats" (*Journal of Heredity,* Vol. 84:170–172, 1993), a "syndrome of caudal anomalies" that include deformed hind legs, twisted pelvis, anal problems and persistent diarrhea and constipation. Robinson is the first to study a relatively large sample of Manx subjects from which he drew his conclusions. The British Manx catteries reported on 412 kittens while the United States survey included 495. The data are broken down by incidences of reported health problems by various tail lengths, or, as Robinson describes it, "tail deformity," thus perpetuating the negative stereotyping of Manx cats as mutants. Although Robinson's test sample is fairly large, missing in the data is any comparison of anomalies produced by Manx cats versus other breeds or the cat population at large. All of the problems associated with the Manx gene as listed in the survey conclusions are problems that can be found in randomly bred cats as well as in other breeds. After reading Robinson's study, it still isn't clear whether the described anomalies are more prevalent in

Manx than in other cats. Robinson does indicate, however, that the health problems listed are more often found in rumpy Manx than in risers, stumpies, or tailed Manx.

The Manx gene is found in the heterozygous condition in all Manx cats (see pages 94–96). Kittens that inherit the Manx gene from both parents fail to develop in the womb, giving rise to the term lethal gene. Although the lethal aspect to the Manx gene was previously established statistically, the moribund fetuses have been detected in the womb as early as the first five weeks of gestation. Manx that are carried to term do not carry any lethal characteristics that would reduce their longevity.

While past bad breeding practices and lack of understanding of the Manx gene and how it functions may have resulted in certain health problems in the Manx cat, research is sketchy and conclusions are often drawn based on inadequate test samples. Today's ethical breeders have established practices that minimize genetic problems and produce strong, healthy cats. Manx breeders in the United States as well as in Europe are reporting no congenital health problems in their kittens. Although such problems related to the Manx gene may exist, more research needs to be done to adequately determine what those are, as well as incidence of occurrence compared with occurrence in other breeds and in the cat population as a whole. Most genetic health problems, regardless of breed, are detectable during the first four months of life, which is why responsible breeders insist on keeping their kittens until they have reached that age before allowing them to be placed in new homes.

Tail Docking

The absence of a tail is what makes the Manx cat's appearance so unusual, and it is what fanciers find most appealing. Although Manx have other interesting qualities, such as their round, cuddly shape and easygoing personalities, Manx lovers want something that looks different from other people's cats, plain and simple. To reconcile that fact with the numbers of kittens born in Manx litters that may be endowed with the final appendage (as well as solve other potential problems that result from the presence of a tail), Manx breeders customarily dock the tails of kittens born with full tails or stumps to make them more attractive to buyers.

In addition to increasing the tailed Manx kittens' marketability, docking tails also helps prevent certain health and behavior problems that can crop up among Manx cats with tails. The Manx gene is a tail modifier gene, and it may cause vertebrae in the tail to fuse and become immobile. Docking removes any potential for long-term health problems arising from

fused vertebrae in the tail. Sometimes, arthritis in tailed Manx cats causes the entire tail to stiffen. In addition, breeding females with fused vertebrae or stiffened tails may not be able to move their tails aside to accept males for mating. The Manx is built to be balanced without a tail, and the presence of a tail destroys that balance. Removing the stump or tail enables the Manx to stand with its hind legs raised, the way a Manx should stand according to breed standard, and walk with a beautiful gait. If the tail is not removed until the cat reaches adulthood, the docking surgery is more painful and traumatic.

The Butt of Pranks

There are behavioral and psychological reasons to remove the extra appendage as well. Breeders attest to the fact that, in a household of cats without tails, the tailed kitten is often picked on by the cats with no tails. Kittens of any breed or variety often attack and play with each other's tails, so a tailed cat in a household of tailless wonders may be the target of the other cats' pranks and amusement. Some breeders call it "tail trauma," and think it inhibits proper development of the Manx kitten's personality because the tailed kitten is always at a disadvantage.

Manx breeders dock the kittens' tails at three to five days of age. Some breeders use orthodontic bands to remove the tails. Banding tails to remove them is a method used by farmers to dock the tails of sheep. The bands are put on the kittens' tails at birth. Kittens have little or no feeling in their tails, so they aren't even aware the band is on. The band cuts off the circulation to the tail, which falls off on its own.

Some breeders will indicate to a buyer that a kitten's tail has been docked, while others don't. Manx kittens that have had their tails docked will be sold as pet quality kittens. Although Manx cats whose tails have been docked can't be shown as Manx in championship competition, they can be shown as household pets. Docked Manx routinely become part of breeding programs to add strength as can Manx cats whose tails have not been docked, assuming all other aspects of conformation to breed standard are present.

Where to Shop

Now that you've decided that you want to buy a Manx kitten or cat and have determined what kind of Manx you want, you need to find a reputable breeder from whom you can purchase a healthy Manx cat as your companion. Finding a reputable breeder will take some effort and research on your part. Before you start looking, a few words about what makes a breeder "reputable" are in order. Unlike the casual or random breeder who simply wants to produce a litter of kittens for all the wrong reasons (e.g., "I want my children to see the miracle of birth" or "I want my female to experience having a litter before I spay her") or the backyard breeder who continually produces kittens, often in deplorable conditions, as a money-making endeavor with little concern about their health and well-being or their conformity to breed standards, reputable breeders are actively engaged in the cat fancy and showing their cats. A reputable breeder will belong to one or more of the pedigreed cat registries (see "Resources") and, by entering their cats in championships, will learn how well the cats he or she produces conform to the standard for the breed. Rep-

utable breeders socialize their cats and kittens and can produce cats of known temperaments that will make them good, people-oriented companions.

A reputable breeder will produce sound, healthy kittens and is concerned for the kittens' welfare. Unlike backyard breeders who sell their kittens through pet stores to buyers they will never meet, reputable breeders want to make certain their kittens are placed in good homes with responsible owners who will provide them with continued quality care. A reputable breeder will be just as concerned about the home you can provide as you are about the quality of the kitten you purchase.

No one can guarantee that a kitten or cat you buy will be free of medical problems for its entire life, but buying your Manx from an established breeder will go a long way in ensuring that the Manx you purchase will be healthy, free of contagious diseases and, with proper care from you, live a long time. A responsible breeder is committed to ethical breeding and to producing healthy, well-adjusted kittens. He or she will provide a written sales contract that describes the terms of sale, a spay/neuter agreement for every cat that is not intended to be part of a breeding program, and a health guarantee that includes assurance that your kitten is free from feline leukemia virus (FLV) and feline immunodeficiency virus (FIV). Many breeders offer buyers a purchase price refund if the kitten's health is deemed unsatisfactory upon being checked by a veterinarian. The contract also may specify that you keep your Manx indoors. A reputable breeder will supply you with the kitten's health and vaccination records and encourage you to visit a veterinarian soon after purchase for an examination. The breeder

Purchasing a Manx from a reputable breeder will help ensure that you find a healthy cat such as this cream tabby-and-white Manx.

Shows and Catteries

One of the best ways to find breeders is by attending cat shows. By talking to Manx breeders, you will be able to learn about the breed disposition and conformity to standard as well as general information on cat care, genetics, and showing. Before buying, visit several shows and look at show quality as well as pet quality Manx. And, don't be afraid to ask questions.

If there are no Manx cats at shows you attend, ask the club sponsoring the show for referrals to Manx breeders in your area. If there are none, you may have to travel some distance to a cattery or do your shopping long distance through other means. You will find breeders listed in the major cat magazines such as *Cat Fancy* and *Cats*. Both are available at newsstands. Contact the purebred cat associations (see page 100) for lists of Manx breeders in your area.

The Cattery Call

Once you have identified some breeders, call them and ask to visit their catteries. The surroundings should be clean, and, for proper socialization, the kittens should have been raised in the breeder's home, not in small or inadequate cages, although pregnant or nurs-

also will provide you with the certificates of registration, which you must complete and send to the association to complete the registration process for your kitten. Some breeders will require proof of neutering before they will send the kitten's registration form to you as buyer (see pages 81–83).

A reputable breeder also will offer advice and assistance if you want to become involved in the cat fancy as an exhibitor, or, once you have learned the ropes, as a breeder. He or she will want to hear from you after you have purchased your Manx and will answer any questions you may have about your new cat and its care.

This lovely brown and white tabby longhair Manx is the result of a sound breeding program.

ing females and kittens may be segregated from the other cats in the household.

Many of the purebred cat associations, such as the CFA and The International Cat Association (ICA), have cattery inspection programs that are intended to separate the cattery wheat from the chaff and to provide the buyer with a quick way to evaluate potential sellers. If you read the breeder ads in the cat magazines or check their home pages on the Web, you will notice that those who have who have passed the inspection list their catteries as "CFA Cattery of Excellence" or "CFA Approved Cattery," for example. Inspection programs vary somewhat from registry to registry. Breeders request inspections from the registry, for which they pay a fee.

Catteries are inspected by licensed veterinarians and must meet stringent criteria to be labeled as a Cattery of Excellence. A veterinarian examines the facility for cleanliness, ventilation, size, condition, and amount and quality of food. He or she also checks the condition of the cats themselves, including weight, coats, presence of parasites, and level of socialization. The cattery

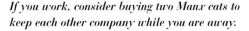

If you work, consider buying two Manx cats to keep each other company while you are away.

inspection approval ratings relate to the overall condition of the cattery, but do not guarantee the health of the individual cats. The inspection must be performed annually for the cattery to continue to receive the approval ratings.

When you purchase a purebred cat, you will be obtaining a companion with which you will spend your time for many years to come. You also will be spending a good deal of money on your choice. You will want to talk to several breeders before deciding from whom you want to purchase your Manx. Interviewing each of them will be an important way to evaluate the catteries and the animals they have available. Once you have conducted your interview, visit the catteries and handle the kittens and cats that interest you. Be aware that you may not see the entire cattery, but you will see enough of the environment to determine under what conditions the cats are raised and whether they are healthy.

Questions to Ask a Seller

When you contact a breeder, be prepared with a list of questions. Conducting a telephone interview will help you find a responsible breeder from whom to buy your Manx cat. Take notes so that you can compare data and choose some catteries to visit.

What are your breeding priorities? The health and temperament of their Manx kittens and cats should be one of the breeders' major priorities. You are entitled to a cat that has a good personality and is physically sound.

The breeder should be actively involved in showing. By competing in the show ring, breeders learn how well their cats conform to the breed standard.

What inoculations have the kittens had? Kittens sold at between 12 and 16 weeks should have received a three-way series of shots called FVRCP—feline viral rhinotracheitis, calicivirus, and panleukopenia.

Do you provide a health guarantee? You should expect to buy a healthy cat that comes from a long line of healthy stock and is free of contagious disease. Breeders may guarantee the health of their kittens and offer to refund your purchase price if the cat is found to have health problems within a specified time after sale.

What associations do you register and exhibit with and why? Different pedigreed cat registries handle breeding differently. Some allow hybridization to achieve various colors such as the colorpoint varieties, which indicate cross-breeding with Siamese or another breed that has colorpoint colors. In the CFA, for example, the Manx stud books are closed; this means that cats of unknown ancestry cannot be brought into their foundation. CFA also will not accept cross-registry without showing a certified pedigree from any other American registries whereas other American registries will accept cross-registry from CFA. If you want to show within CFA, you need to find a breeder who registers his or her kittens with CFA. If you want a pet cat and showing is not something you see in your future, then the association to which the breeder belongs may not be an issue.

Do you operate a Cattery of Excellence? Several associations operate cattery inspection programs. Breeders whose catteries pass the inspections are proud of their ratings and want to share that information with buyers. A Cattery of Excellence rating does not guarantee the health of the animals found in the cattery, however, and it does not constitute an endorsement of the cattery by the registry granting the rating.

How long have you been breeding? In the world of cat breeding, longevity is a sign of experience and proven track records. Breeders who have been breeding for 20 years or more can give you a good indication of the longevity of their cats and offspring. If a breeder has less than five years of experience, ask with whom he or she works and how much breeding experience the other person has.

What awards have the parents won? The breeder should provide the buyer with a pedigree that will indicate the show classifications (Champion, Grand Champion, Distinguished Merit) as well as NW (National Winner) and RW (Regional Winner) of the kittens' parents and grandparents. If you plan to show your Manx, knowing that it comes from winning stock that conforms in every way to breed standards is an indication that the cat's offspring are more likely to produce champions.

May I visit? You will learn a lot by visiting the breeder. Are the surroundings clean and do the cats look healthy and well cared for?

Can you send me a picture of the kitten? If you are a serious buyer, the breeder may send you a photo of available kittens. Many Manx breeders maintain Web pages with photos of cats and kittens on them, so, if you can't get to the breeder, ask if he or she has a presence on the Web.

Do you have any references? Reputable breeders want to place kittens in good homes, and take pride in happy customers. If you are committed to purchase, ask potential sellers if they can provide you with two or three names of people to whom they've sold kittens.

Questions Breeders May Ask You

Reputable breeders have invested substantial time and energy to produce and raise sound, healthy kittens, and they will want to make certain that you are able to provide a good home to their offspring before they sell a kitten to you. Expect the breeder to ask you questions before the sale takes place, and don't be offended. The breeder is simply trying to find out what kind of pet parent you will be and determine what kind of Manx kitten or cat will best satisfy your needs.

What kind of Manx do you want, and how much do you know about the Manx breed? A breeder may try to determine how much thought you have given to the kind of cat you want and the amount of research you have done into the Manx breed.

What does your family unit consist of? A cat with a placid personality might be more appropriate for a family with children or seniors than an energetic cat. The breeder also will want to know if any children in the family have been taught how to properly handle a kitten or cat.

What is your life like? A breeder may want to know if you travel frequently, work late, or are involved in extracurricular activities to determine how much time the cat may be spending alone. If you frequently work late, the breeder may recommend that you buy two cats to keep each other company.

Do you have any cats or other pets? A breeder will want to know about other cats or pets you have in the household and how well they get along. If the breeder has other pets as well, he or she may suggest a cat or kitten that gets along particularly well with the other animals.

What kinds of cats did you have previously and what happened to them? A breeder will want to know what might have happened to your previous cats. Did they live to a ripe old age? Were they given up for adoption? What happened to them if a baby came along? The breeder should stress that purchasing a cat will be a long-term commitment, not just a passing fancy.

Will you keep your Manx indoors? Veterinarians and animal behaviorists these days consider an indoor environment the safest place for a cat to live. Breeders want to ensure the safest possible environment for the kittens and cats they sell.

Shopping for your Manx will take some time and effort, but it also should be an enjoyable experience—one that ushers in a long-term relationship you will have with your Manx companion.

PREPARING FOR THE ARRIVAL OF YOUR MANX

The Basics

When you bring your Manx home, you will want to spend as much time with it as possible. Having basic necessities on hand when you arrive with your Manx will help ensure that you spend the first few days getting to know your Manx and letting your Manx get to know you.

Among the items your Manx will need to have on hand are food and water bowls. You will find many styles of bowls in a variety of prices in your local pet store. Choose one that is large and wide enough that your Manx is able to eat or drink without crushing its whiskers against the sides. Bowls should be curved so that food does not slide out onto the floor as your cat is licking it. Food and water bowls should be separate and they should be sturdy enough that they don't tip over. Glass, metal, or ceramic bowls are preferable to plastic ones, which retain oils. Plastic bowls may contribute to feline acne—black, crusty patches on a cat's chin.

An Important Purchase

A litterbox is another necessary item that you must have on hand immediately for your Manx's use. Imagine moving to a new home and finding that the bathrooms were out of order or that there were none! Although you would seek the nearest public restroom, your Manx might seek the nearest location in your house to perform its bodily functions. Having a box with filler will help prevent accidents from occurring. Litterboxes come in all sizes and shapes, from the simplest boxes that look like dishpans to the most complex waste removal systems that clean themselves as soon as the cat steps out. Some boxes have hoods; others have high sides to prevent litter from scattering as a cat digs and buries its wastes. A Manx is a medium-sized cat, so choose a box in which it can comfortably turn around.

Choosing Litter

In addition to the box, you will need a supply of litter. If you thought selecting a box was complicated, wait till you shop for litter, which comes in many types, from the clay litter that has been on the market for many years to the newer clumping litter that makes waste removal easier for the owner. There are also many environment-friendly litters made from materials such as newspaper, wood chips, and corn husks. Some can be flushed down the toilet. Others must be bagged and put out with the trash for pickup. Kitty's wastes must be removed daily, so purchase a heavy plastic litter scoop with a molded handle.

Your Manx will have been taught to use the litterbox while at the home of the breeder from whom you purchased it. Place the litterbox in your Manx's room when you first bring it home and show your Manx where the box is. That is all it takes. When your Manx is acclimated to your home, choose a spot for the litter box that is convenient for both of you and one that is quiet and out of the way so that your Manx won't be disturbed while using its facilities.

Creature Comforts

Cats, as a general rule, spend up to 16 hours a day sleeping. That amount of time may increase as a cat ages. Manx, like all cats, seek out the places that are most comfortable to snooze, and those places might include your upholstered furniture or your bed. You may want your Manx to sleep wherever it wants, but providing your Manx with a bed to call its own will help increase its comfort level and may, in fact, cut down on the hair it deposits elsewhere. Cat beds, like litterboxes,

come in many styles and sizes in price ranges to fit every pocketbook. Some are simple padded cushions while others may be small pieces of furniture designed to complement your decor. A favorite among cats at cat shows are the small, rounded, fake fur kitty cups in which cats can curl up and snuggle.

Cats Will Scratch

Your Manx will come with its claws intact, and you will want to keep them that way if you plan to exhibit. Cats keep their claws sharp, and remove the old nail sheaths, as new ones grow, by scratching. Animal behaviorists also believe that cats scratch to mark territories with scent glands on the pads of their feet. Whatever the reason, cats want and need to scratch, so providing your Manx with something on which to work its claws will help it do what comes naturally and help you keep your furniture from being shredded. Purchasing a scratch post or two is a good way to direct your Manx to the appropriate place when it must do its nails. Posts come in many sizes, shapes, and materials. They can be freestanding, or attached to window ledges or doorknobs. Some are elaborate climbing apparatuses that provide a cat with a home gym on which to exercise as well as scratch. A post with a variety of scratching surfaces that include carpet, sisal, and wood is ideal. Cats are naturally drawn to scratch posts, but if you have

Choose a litterbox large enough for your Manx to turn around in.

some convincing to do, sprinkle a little catnip on the post to attract your Manx.

Even though cats have been domesticated for 5,000 years, *felis catus* retains many of its hunting skills. Although you will be keeping your Manx indoors, you will need to provide it with an outlet for those skills by offering playthings that enable your Manx to practice its instinctive behavior. Playing with your Manx is also an important bonding activity and a good way to help it keep fit and healthy. Toys need not be elaborate or expensive. Cats enjoy anything that moves, so a crumpled paper ball or plastic practice golf ball to chase will provide it with hours of fun. Manx cats often learn to retrieve, so you may find your Manx bringing its toys to you to initiate a game. A popular toy is a plastic rod with some feathers or pieces of fabric attached to it with fishing line.

Safety First

Remove small parts or bells from toys before offering them to your Manx. If swallowed, they can injure your Manx's stomach or intestinal tract. Catnip, an herb with a pungent aroma that has a positive effect on most cats, might help your Manx to feel at home in its new home.

If you have trouble finding exactly what you want for your Manx locally, look in catalogs, the classified sections of the major cat magazines (see page 101), or product vendors at cat shows.

Cat-Proofing Your Home

Cats are naturally curious animals, and your Manx will want to explore every nook and cranny in your home. Cats, like kids, don't always know what is good for them, so you will have to make sure that nothing in your house poses a potential danger to your new cat companion.

Some cats are chewers. Exposed electrical wires may present a danger if you discover that your Manx enjoys sinking its teeth into them.

A few items to pick up before you bring your Manx home.

A Stumpie Manx cat on the Isle of Man.

The saying, "curiosity killed the cat," has a basis in truth, so a good way to prevent your Manx from succumbing to its inquisitiveness is to secure your electrical wires inside heavy-duty plastic strips designed to conceal cords that travel across the floors in office cubicles. These strips come in many colors and have a slit in one side into which to slip the wire. They can be laid across a floor, up a wall, or along a baseboard. Another option is to rub

Manx love to play, even as adults, so have some toys available for your new Manx.

A sweet expression is one of the things that makes a Manx so appealing.

a substance such as tabasco sauce or eucalyptus oil onto the wires. This must be repeated periodically, however, because the offensive taste or odor dissipates in time.

Keep harmful chemicals and cleaning products out of your Manx's reach. If you've used the products to clean your house, make sure you remove any residue that your Manx might walk across and subsequently lick off its paws or hair. Cats are attracted to automobile antifreeze and enjoy drinking it. Antifreeze is lethal, so clean up any that has spilled where your Manx might come into contact with it. Don't assume that your Manx is safe because you've purchased an antifreeze product that claims to be pet-friendly. Pet-friendly antifreeze can still kill; it just takes more of it to cause harm.

Know Your Plants

Many plants are poisonous to cats, and they can cause symptoms that range from vomiting and diarrhea to convulsions and death. Some of these poisonous plants are common houseplants, and you may have them in your home. There are too many plants to list here, but if you are unsure, ask your veterinarian. To obtain a complete list of plants, both toxic and nontoxic, including their scientific names and associated problems or hazards, write to the

The handsome brown tabby longhaired Manx is one of many free-roaming Manx that populate the Isle of Man.

Visit your veterinarian soon after you acquire your kitten.

gency before finding a veterinarian with whom you can establish rapport. If the breeder is local, ask him or her for a recommendation. Ask fellow cat lovers you know or work with why they like their veterinarians. Don't feel obligated to take your Manx to the first veterinarian you contact. Be willing to shop around to find one who is familiar with Manx and willing to spend time talking to you about your cat's condition.

National Animal Poison Control Center (see Information, page 100). Enclose a check for $10, payable to the NAPCC.

Keep all human medications out of reach of your Manx, and do not give any of your medications to your Manx unless advised to do so by your veterinarian. Cats are smaller than humans and have a much different body chemistry. If you've dropped a pill, make sure you find it and pick it up before your Manx does and decides to have it as a snack or play with it like a toy.

Finding a Veterinarian

After you purchase your Manx kitten or cat, make an appointment with a veterinarian for an examination. Buying from a responsible breeder will go a long way in ensuring that you have obtained a healthy cat, but you don't want to wait until you have an emer-

Visit the Clinic

One of the best ways to evaluate a veterinarian is to visit his or her animal hospital or clinic. Take note of what you see. Is the waiting room clean and tidy? Are office personnel courteous and helpful or do they seem too busy to bother? Is there a separate waiting area for cats? Animals may become stressed at the veterinary clinic, and barking dogs sitting next to frightened, shivering cats can add a level of anxiety that may affect the veterinarian's diagnosis. Ask to see the hospital area. Is it clean or cluttered? Are dogs and cats housed separately or together? Is there an isolation ward for cats with contagious illnesses?

Make an appointment to interview the veterinarian and prepare a list of questions ahead of time. Ask what the clinic's hours are and if evening and weekend appointments are available. How does the veterinarian handle emergencies and off-hours problems? If your cat needs treatment right away, will you be able to get to see the veterinarian in a reasonable amount of time? Ask for the veterinarian's credentials. Becoming a veterinarian requires that a person have a college degree and at least three years study in an accredited veterinary school.

What's in a Name?

All veterinary schools except the University of Pennsylvania, which confers a Veterinary Medical Degree (VMD) offer a Doctor of Veterinary Medicine (DVM) degree. VMD and DVM are essentially the same, and you should not make a decision based on which one a potential veterinarian holds. Veterinarians must be licensed in the state in which they practice. To keep abreast of current veterinary medical trends, veterinarians join professional associa-tions such as the American Veterinary Medical Association or the American Association of Feline Practitioners.

When you interview a veterinarian, be respectful of his or her time. Take a pen and paper so you can write down the responses to your questions and make notes about what you see. After you've selected a veterinarian, take your Manx for a visit and assessment of its physical condition. The veterinarian will begin a history on it, so that if an emergency arises, he or she will not be in the dark about your cat. If your cat does become ill, be willing to describe to your veterinarian what symptoms you've observed. Be as detailed as possible about what has occurred and when the symptoms began. Your relationship with your veterinarian will last a long time. Next to you, your veterinarian will be the most important person in your cat's life.

BRINGING HOME YOUR MANX CAT OR KITTEN

Transporting Your Manx

If you intend to travel by automobile to a cattery to find the perfect Manx, bringing it home will be relatively easy. Purchase a sturdy carrier made of hard plastic or fiberglass with holes for ventilation in the sides. Newer models have the opening in the top instead of the front, so it is easy to move a cat in and out of the carrier. Some models even have wheels and a long handle so they can be pulled rather than lifted. These are especially handy for cat owners who have back problems or difficulty bending over. If you are purchasing a kitten, obtain a carrier that is large enough to accommodate an adult cat, so you won't have to purchase a larger carrier as the cat grows.

Cats travel with varying degrees of acceptance, so you may find your Manx serenading you to express its dissatisfaction during the trip home. You can avoid stress by providing the cat or kitten with a familiar article of clothing or bedding from the breeder on which it can lie in the carrier. If the trip home is longer than five or six hours, place in the carrier a shallow cardboard box for litter and a sturdy water bowl that won't tip over. It is advisable not to feed your Manx right before and during travel unless the trip requires that you stay overnight somewhere. Before assuming that your Manx will be welcome at a hotel, phone ahead to verify that they allow pets. Many of the larger hotel chains do, but they like to know in advance if their guests will be bringing along four-footed family members.

Plan Ahead

When traveling in warm weather, make sure that the car has air-conditioning or adequate ventilation and don't leave your Manx unattended inside the car if you must make a rest stop *en route*. Automobile interiors reach temperatures of 120°F (88°C) or more in a very short time. A vented window is not enough to ensure good circulation of air. Animals left inside parked cars can suffocate and die quickly. If you must stop for more than a few minutes, take your Manx with you.

If you are traveling by air to pick up your dream cat, you also will need a carrier even if you intend to take your cat aboard the airplane with you. Airlines that allow cats in the passenger compartment require that they be kept in a carrier under the seat. Contact the airlines to find out if cats are allowed on board with you and to determine the carrier dimensions required. Soft padded fabric carriers slide easily under the seat, but they are not as well ventilated as the hard-sided carriers and do not protect a cat from accidental kicking or falling objects. Transporting your Manx in a sturdy carrier in the airplane's luggage compartment is another option. Many pet owners have done this successfully, and airlines have come a long way in making sure that animals have adequate heat and ventilation on the trip. If you feel more secure keeping kitty with you, placing it in an airline-approved carrier under the seat in front of you is the way to go.

Welcome Home

You'll want to bestow on your Manx as much attention and love as you can, and your Manx will be ready and willing to accept it as well as love you back. But before buying your Manx, consider the time of year and what else might be occurring in your household. Will you have the time that is needed to get to know your cat and the time to allow it to get to know you? Holidays, for example, mean a lot of hustle and bustle, and extra demands often make it difficult to find the time needed to spend with a new pet. Is the household experiencing any type of disruption? Carpet installation or house painting might require your attention, leaving kitty to amuse itself. Family members moving out or in might confuse a cat trying to adjust to its new surroundings. Try to choose a stable time to bring home your Manx companion.

Your Manx may appear a little nervous or stressed when it first arrives in its new home. Consider: Your Manx has just left the security and safety of its first home. It no longer has the people or other animals with whom it felt comfortable. It may react to stress by refusing food, vomiting, having diarrhea, becoming constipated, or hiding. In spite of how wonderful your home is and how much you love your new cat, your Manx may need a little extra tender loving care to help it adjust.

A Room of Its Own

The best way to reduce the stress your Manx may feel about having been plucked out of a familiar environment and brought into a strange one is to allow your Manx the opportunity to learn about you, your family, and your home gradually. This is especially important if you've purchased a kitten that may feel overwhelmed at first. Permit your Manx cat or kitten to explore and become familiar with your house a little at a time. If your house is a large one and has lots of activity, your new Manx may feel more relaxed having a place to call its own to get away from any commotion that may occur. Select a room that is the cat's place for the first week or two. Place a food and water bowl, litterbox and kitty necessities such as a bed, scratch post, and toys in the room. Ask the breeder if you could take a little plastic bag of litter with you to sprinkle on top of your cat's

Your Manx will feel safe and secure in its own crate.

new litter so it smells familiar and encourages your kitten to use its box. Spend time in the room playing with, talking to, and grooming your cat. When you feel that it is beginning to bond with you, allow the cat out into the rest of the house for short periods of time. As the cat's comfort level increases, extend the time. Cats are curious creatures, and you will find your Manx ready and eager to explore its new domain.

Pheromone Facts

A product that was developed to help stop cat's spraying was also found to help promote exploratory behavior and initiate eating when cats are in new environments, such as a new home, a kennel, a cage at a veterinary hospital or clinic, or the benching cage at a cat show. It was developed in France, where scientists identified common feline facial pheromones, which cats secrete through cheek glands and deposit when they rub against objects. Studies showed cats that were given the pheromones began exploring new environments approximately twice as rapidly as cats that were not given them. Available in spray bottles through veterinarians, the product contains facial pheromones, which when sprayed around the room at your cat's level, helps it feel comfortable in new places. If you would like to give your Manx a jump start in acclimating to its new home, discuss with your veterinarian the option of using the pheromone spray.

Teach your children to be gentle with their new pet.

Proper Introductions

Once you have isolated your Manx, and it has had a chance to relax from the trip and explore its temporary quarters, you can begin to introduce it to other members of the household. Manx usually get along well with everyone in the family and their calm dispositions enable them to acclimate well to dogs and some other pets. Proper introductions will go a long way toward ensuring the success of any relationships that need to be established.

Children and Cats

If you have small children, instruct them how to properly handle the cat. Most injuries to children that involve animals are due to a lack of understanding on the part of the child of how to approach, pick up, or pet the animal. If your child approaches the cat with too much exuberance or energy or tries to pick up the cat by the front legs, for example, the cat may not understand the child's intentions and may feel it must defend itself with its claws or teeth. As a result, the child may be scratched or bitten and become afraid of the cat instead of benefiting from

the love and affection the cat can offer. In addition to posing potential harm to the child, mishandling poses a threat to the animal. In spite of the Manx's sturdy, muscular build, it is still a cat and therefore a delicate creature requiring a tender touch, especially when it is a kitten. Bring your children into your Manx's room, one at a time. Make sure your child is seated. Allow your child to offer the cat treats. Ask your child to sit

This attractive young black and white Manx (top) is called a tuxedo because it looks as if it is dressed up for a formal occasion. Manx come in all colors and patterns, including tabby (right) and solid colors such as these two handsome cats (below), one white and one black.

still for a few minutes while your cat smells and investigates your child. If your Manx is a kitten, place it in your child's lap and allow your child to stroke it gently.

Other Pets

Just as it's important to allow your cat to get to know its surroundings and human family members gradually, it is also essential to let your cat gradually meet other pets in the household. There is no magic formula that will tell you whether a cat will have success

with other animal family members. Some cats like other cats, dogs, and other animals. Some don't. Some dogs or other animals will enjoy the company of members of species to which they don't belong. Some won't. Compatibility is as much an individual animal's preference as it is a species-centered one. If you've purchased your Manx from a breeder, you already know that it is accustomed to living with other cats. If you are bringing a cat into a household with other pets such as dogs or birds, it might be useful to know ahead of time whether the cat or kitten you are interested in purchasing has had exposure to those types of animals. Animals of different species can adapt to each other, but it is best accomplished when they are young. The chances for success at interspecies relationships are greater if you adopt a kitten rather than an adult cat, provided that the other species, such as a dog, poses no threat to the kitten. If the animals in question are of

different sizes or temperaments, be sure they are compatible and that none of them becomes injured. Your budgie may look like breakfast to your cat if it is unaccustomed to living in close proximity to birds. On the other hand, your pet cockatoo may maim your Manx if it gets too close when you're not there. If you have small mammals such as gerbils, mice, or hamsters, make sure they are adequately protected and out of kitty's reach, and keep the aquarium covered for the safety of both cat and fish.

Resident Dog

When introducing a new cat to a resident dog, allow them to learn about each other by scent. To prevent fearful imprinting on a new cat or kitten, never take it and hold it up to the established animal, whether it be canine or feline. If the newcomer learns to fear the other animal in the house, alleviating the fear may take months or even years, and inappropriate behaviors that are equally difficult to correct may result. A useful technique to make the homecoming happy is to place the animals' food bowls on each side of the door to the new cat's quarters and allow them to partake of a meal in close proximity. Since eating is something they enjoy, the two animals will associate a pleasant activity with each other. After the animals have investigated each other through closed doors, allow them to interact for brief periods in a controlled setting. If you are introducing your Manx to a resident dog, leash the dog and allow it into the cat's room. Command the dog to sit or stay. You will be able to tell quickly how the dog will respond to the cat and vice versa. If your Manx wants to hide, let it.

Don't force the issue. If it appears interested and curious about the dog, allow it to investigate, but continue to keep the dog leashed and unable to lunge and frighten the cat. Offer them treats to help ease tension. During the introductory period, keep the socialization short and under your guidance. Once they are familiar with each other, allow the two pets to interact without your presence.

Cat Combo

If your resident pet is a cat, the same techniques apply. Cats are more social than they have been given credit for, and many a multi-cat owner or breeder will attest to the fact that two or more cats can and do peacefully coexist under the same roof. Pecking orders among domestic cats in a group is fluid rather than linear as it is in packs of dogs. The order in the feline hierarchy may be determined not only by which cat has arrived first on the scene, but also by the cat's sex, age, personality, and whether it has borne a litter of kittens. Because of the complexity of factors affecting the feline hierarchy, you will have an easier time slipping a newcomer in than if the hierarchy were rigidly defined. In spite of this, you will want to offer your resident cat as much, if not more, of your time, attention, and affection during the introductory period as you do the newcomer.

During the introductory process, allow both cats to smell each other's belongings,

If properly introduced, Manx get along well with other pets.

such as bedding and toys. Rub a towel on one cat and rub it over the other and *vice versa* to mix scents. Place their dishes on each side of the door. Allow some play time on each side of the door. Play is a wonderful bonding activity, so the more you play with both cats together during their initial introductions, the closer they will become. When you first allow the newcomer to have access to the rest of the house for brief periods of time, put the resident cat in the newcomer's room to smell and investigate it. Your two cats may not like each other immediately, so expect some hissing and growling. Be patient and allow them the time to accept one another. Compatibility may take days, weeks, or even months. Be sure to allow both cats the choice of a place to hide or seek refuge. Until you are sure that the cats can coexist peacefully, keep them separated when you are not at home.

Manx Birthplace

The Isle of Man, reputedly the birthplace of the Manx breed, is in the middle of the Irish Sea, midway between Liverpool, England, and Belfast, Ireland. The Isle of Man encompasses 227 square miles (588 km) of what is primarily rural countryside, its major cities being along its 100 mile (161 km) coastline. It is 32 miles (51.5 km) long at its longest point and 13 miles (30 km) wide at its widest point. The Isle's territory includes the Calf of Man, a small island at the southwestern extremity of the Isle, from which it is separated by a narrow strait of water known as the Calf Sound. The major activity on the Isle of Man is tourism, and, in addition to the Manx cat, the Isle is famous for its Tourist Trophy Motorcycle races that are held each May and June; it is also celebrated as the birthplace of the Bee Gees singing group.

UNDERSTANDING YOUR MANX

A Walk on the Wild Side

On the evolutionary scale, man has sustained a relationship with the cat for a relatively short period of time. He saw the practicality of domesticating cattle, pigs, and dogs long before he ever found a need for *felis catus*. Estimates for the beginning of the symbiotic pairing range from 3,000 to 5,000 years ago. It was the ancient Egyptians whose perspicacity and appreciation for grace and beauty led them to investigate the mutually beneficial alliance between human and cat. If cats kept the royal granaries free of rodents, the Egyptian powers-that-be would allow them to eat freely, adorn their households, pose for sculptures—and be sacrificed, mummified, and buried in royal graves with their deceased owners. What animal could ask for more?

The wild cat that is believed to be the predecessor of today's domestic cat in all its many iterations was a small cat known as *felis libyca*, native to the area of northern Africa of which ancient Egypt was a part. Just slightly larger than today's feline model—10 to 18 pounds (4.5 to 8 kg)—*felis libyca* is a light brown, striped, or spotted cat that is found as far east as India. Images of Egyptian cats found in frescoes and tomb paintings bear a striking resemblance to *felis libyca*.

All behavior is based on an animal's genetics and the environment in which it lives. As a result of their brief domestic history, cats still retain some of the instinctive behaviors found in their wild cousins. Given the opportunity, most cats will hunt, claim, and defend territories, and participate in mating rituals that, when heard during the wee hours of the night, can make the blood of even the most devoted cat owner run cold. Your purebred Manx, the result of a careful and reputable breeding program, will exhibit those behaviors minimally inside your home as long as you provide an indoor outlet for its natural drives and have it spayed or neutered to reduce its sexual urges (see pages 90–91).

How Cats Communicate

Although long considered to be independent, today's domestic cat relies on its human companion to provide for its needs and wants. To that end, the cat has refined its communication skills to accomplish its goals while still retaining some of the behaviors inherited from its wild ancestors. As most cat owners will attest, it takes a cat companion little time to wrap its owner around its paw.

Long thought to be solitary because the act of hunting takes place through individual effort rather than in family groups, cats are quite social and have developed a whole range of communication methods that help define their roles in social hierarchies. Cats living outdoors form social groups—usually around food sources—mate, and reproduce. The hierarchy of a pack of cats is not as rigid in structure as in a pack of dogs. Although behaviorists have long felt that there was no alpha cat that leads the group as there is an alpha dog in a pack, some are questioning that concept. As with a pack of dogs, there is, at times, the equivalent of an omega dog—a cat that has the lowest status and tries unsuccessfully to become a *bona fide* member of the group. Within a group of cats, an ostracized animal is what animal behaviorists call a pariah—a cat that is constantly tormented and picked on by the others in the group until it leaves to live a solitary life.

Indoors, the pariah cat does not have that option and depends on its human caregiver to create a situation in which it can function. Even so, the feline social structure is more fluid, often dominated by females, especially if the group is made up of cats that have been sexually altered.

Body Language

Cats communicate with their humans in much the same way they communicate with one another. It is estimated that more than 70 percent of human communication is nonverbal, including the written word, facial expressions, and body language. Obviously, cats can't read or write, but your Manx will use body movements and facial expressions to let you know what it wants and how it feels. As your relationship with your Manx deepens, you will come to know what is on its mind just by observing how it carries itself, holds its head, looks at you with those big round eyes, and moves its facial muscles as it responds to you and environmental stimuli. Your Manx, a member of an intelligent and perceptive breed of cat, will come to know you as well. It will

Manx body language:

cautiously alert

fearful

defensive

recognize when you are ill or unhappy and need the emotional lift that stroking a cat and listening to it purr provides; it will know when you are upbeat and in the mood for a good game of fetch, eagerly bringing you a favorite toy to throw. In spite of their wild ancestry and the common traits they share with all species of wild cats, expect your Manx to be an individual with its own personality. How the two of you communicate will depend to a large degree on the environment in which you both live and the level on which you interact. The more attention you give your Manx, the more your Manx will want to communicate with you.

Marksmanship

Cats frequently rub against things. Humans don't often get close enough to wild cats to observe this, but when they are able, they find that the phenomenon is common among wild cats, too. Television and movie star Clarence the Cross-eyed Lion was known to slide against his owner and handler. Cats will rub against inanimate objects, people, and other animals, including cats and dogs in the same household. Animal behaviorists think rubbing is a form of marking. As the cat rubs, it deposits scents that tell other cats a cat has been here.

Marking is a way of saying to another cat, "Fluffy was here," but doesn't seem to have the effect of driving another cat away or putting up a sign that says, "Keep out." Marking behavior serves three functions. Marking other animals in the social group is called allo-marking, which enables members to form a common group odor so they can identify each other. Territorial marking provides some geographic orientation to a cat whether it be indoors or out. Also, marking helps a cat be more confident about where it is.

Things Cats Do

Head butting: Often associated with rubbing is head butting. Although no one is sure why cats do it, head butting can occur between a cat and its person, another cat, or another species, such as the family dog. A cat may butt its head against something and continue the action with a long sideways rub. Whatever the reason, rubbing and head butting are pleasurable experiences to cats, and the act is perceived by cat owners to be one of affection and love. A cat won't claim as part of its territory or butt heads with something it doesn't like—animate or inanimate object, human, or animal—so there is an element of truth to the notion.

Kneading: Another popular activity among cats is kneading with their toes. Kneading is carried over from a cat's first few weeks of life when, as a suckling kitten, it kneaded its mother's stomach to stimulate the flow of

threatening

curious

disdainful

This free-roaming tuxedo Manx on the Isle of Man exhibits a common body posture, raising its posterior as a sign of good will and friendship toward other cats and humans.

milk. Adult cats continue to knead when they feel safe and contented, usually on anything soft, from a comfortable blanket to their owners' abdomens. Cats may distend their nails to varying degrees during this process, so how comfortable the kneading process is may depend on your Manx, the layers of clothing you are wearing, or your ability to withstand sharp toenails digging into your skin. Keeping your Manx's nails clipped will help reduce scratching of your skin when it kneads. Consider kneading a flattering activity, and don't punish your Manx for doing it.

Offense and defense: Defensive and offensive postures are easily read from cat to cat. They occur whenever a cat threatens or feels threatened by other cats, animals, or humans. A defensive cat will try to ward off impending danger by using a host of scare tactics designed to frighten the offender. Its ears will flatten against its head, its pupils will become large and saucer-like, its hair will bristle and stand out, especially along its spine and tail, and it may crouch or stand erect with its head lowered. A frightened cat may hiss and spit to fend off the enemy. The hair on its body will stand out to give the illusion of greater size. A cat with a tail may wrap it securely around its body or may fold it downward.

No one is entirely sure why cats rub against objects, but it is commonly thought to be a way of marking territory.

When a cat goes on the offensive, its body language says, "Get out of my way" or, "You have something I want." A mother cat may act offensively to guard her kittens, or a cat may wish to protect its food or favorite toy. The cat that initiates a spat may emit a low growl from its throat, hiss, and swat its opponent. Its lips may curl back to expose its sharp teeth. Expect a cat on the offensive to appear confident and in control. If you live in a multicat household where the feline group members interact on a daily basis, expect the offensive or defensive activities of your Manx to be at a minimum.

Tail language: On cats that have tails, tail movement is a good indication of how the cat feels. An upright tail is a sign of acceptance and good will. It allows a companion cat access to smelling the anal area. A swishing tail is a sign of annoyance, while a drooping tail is an indication of resignation or despondency. The Manx has been dealt the short end of the stick when it comes to using a tail to reveal emotions, but it will have enough other bodily displays to let you know how it feels.

Your Manx may indicate its pleasure to you by giving love bites—little nibbles as you exchange affection. Love bites are differentiated from aggressive biting by their gentleness and the lack of other bodily postures that indicate when a cat is angry, offensive, or defensive. Your Manx also may enjoy licking you in

the same way it washes itself, its littermates, or its feline companions. Your hair, arms, or face may be targets of your Manx's desire to either impart affection or to give you a bath. Washing is a positive social function engaged in by cats living communally, so it is passed along to

This red classic tabby Manx exhibits a relaxed but alert facial expression.

their human companions when a person replaces the feline members of the group. If your Manx becomes annoyed with you, expect it to sit facing away from you—the feline version of "mooning."

The Eyes Have It

The Manx has large round eyes that are very demonstrative, as are its facial expressions. Manx eye colors are defined in the registry's standard. Your Manx has excellent night vision, and your cat's eyes may appear to glow in the dark as light is reflected from the layer of cells behind the retina called *tapetum lucidum*, which acts like a mirror. In daylight, your Manx's pupils expand and contract, depending on both the amount of ambient light and your cat's mood. Because the cat is a nocturnal hunter, its pupils contract into slits in bright light. This improves visual acuity and depth of field, enabling it to see clearly for greater distances. In dim light, a cat's pupils expand to allow the maximum amount of light to enter its eyes.

Manx cats have no problem conveying their emotions to whomever is watching. A relaxed, alert cat will have wide eyes, ears that are standing straight up, and relaxed facial muscles. When your Manx is feeling especially contented, its eyes are half closed and it has a dreamy expression on its face. The contented cat also may purr and knead.

If your Manx experiences fear or aggression, it will lower its head and tilt its ears forward, and its pupils will enlarge. To another cat, a direct stare is a sign of hostility and dominance, while blinking allows mutual gazing without threat. An angry cat will furrow its brow, constrict its pupils, and tilt its ears slightly down and back. A cat that is being inquisitive will have a somewhat surprised look on its face. It may lean forward on its feet, indicating intense concentration. Its pupils will be slightly dilated and its ears pricked forward to hear the sound that piqued its curiosity.

The Sound of Music

One of the most appealing things about cats is their purring. Listening to a cat purr lowers blood pressure and reduces stress, according to recent studies. Your Manx will purr when it is happy and contented. You also may find your Manx purring when it is nervous or frightened; for example, when you've taken it to your veterinarian's office. Cats even purr when they are dying. Exactly how or why cats purr is still a mystery, but one theory is that purring is caused by the flow of blood through the vena cava, a large vein in the cat's chest cavity. When the muscles contract around the vein, the resulting vibrations produce an air turbulence that creates the purring sound. Purring will accompany many activities in which your Manx engages—sleeping with you, playing, kneading, eating, or simply sitting next to you on the sofa. However cats do it, purring is one of the most soothing sounds in nature.

Cat Talk

Although the Manx is not one of the typically vocal breeds of cats such as the Siamese, you can expect your Manx to verbalize periodically. Just as cats use their bodies to indicate what they want and how they feel, cats also develop a vocal repertoire made up of many different sounds to communicate with their owners just as they communicate with other cats. You can help encourage your Manx's "talking" by speaking to it when your Manx speaks to you. The sound and tone of your voice will be just as soothing to your Manx as its purr is to you, and hearing your voice is one of the ways your Manx will learn about you. Talking to your cat is also one of the ways you will train it to do what you want and not to do what you don't want. Teaching your Manx the meaning of many of the words we use will socialize it and help it adjust to living with humans.

The breeder from whom you purchased your Manx may have given it a name, which you may change if you prefer. Cats easily learn several names and nicknames, so don't worry about your Manx becoming confused if you bestow on it a new name when you bring it home. If you are registering and exhibiting your Manx, you'll give it a name appropriate to its breed and ancestry in addition to a name that you call it at home.

Litterbox Lessons

Cats love to dig, so using a box of filler will draw your Manx like a magnet when it's potty time. A cat typically digs a small hole in the filler, deposits its waste and buries it again, although not every cat follows this ritual (see pages 25–26).

Cats occasionally stop using their litterboxes for a variety of reasons. This can be caused by a health-related problem, so if your Manx urinates or defecates outside its box, have it examined by a veterinarian to rule out physical causes before embarking on a behavior modification program. If your Manx stops using its litterbox, try to remember that it is trying to tell you something about the litterbox itself or something that is happening inside the home.

Stress from the absence of the owner, a new cat in the household, or other environmental causes may induce a cat to urinate or defecate in inappropriate places. When trying to encourage your cat to return to its litterbox, never use physical punishment or rub its nose in its wastes. This will destroy trust and make your cat fear you. The key to solving the problem is patience and a willingness to work with the cat to determine and remove the cause of the difficulty.

One of the most common reasons cats stop using their litterboxes is that removal of wastes does not occur often enough. Cats are fastidious creatures, and, if the litterbox is not clean, they will relieve themselves elsewhere. Scoop the box daily and clean it periodically with a mild detergent or a solution of vinegar and water. The box's location may cause litterbox lapses. If your Manx must pass Fido's bed to get to the litterbox or use it while Junior and his friends are coming in and out of the mud room, your Manx may decide to go elsewhere. Be certain that no one in the house, such as a small child, is disturbing your cat while it is in the litterbox or on its way to it. If your Manx is constantly startled or tormented, it may decide to eliminate its wastes wherever it is convenient or safe.

If you have more than one cat, providing an additional box may be the solution. Behaviorists recommend one litterbox per cat and one extra box. Boxes should be put in more than one location so that your transgressing Manx can find a box easily whenever it needs one. If your Manx urinates and defecates out of its box, it may not like the type of litter. Cats often prefer one type of substrate, so you may have to experiment to find one that your Manx fully appreciates. If your Manx potties in the bathtub, for example, it may mean that your Manx prefers a cool, smooth surface, so providing a box with little or no litter in it may encourage it to return to the correct facilities.

If your Manx has soiled a carpet or other area of the house, you must discourage it from returning there to urinate. Blot the area dry and clean it with a mild detergent or vinegar and water solution. Apply a good commercial odor neutralizer to the spot. Cat shows are a good place to find quality odor neutralizing products that are sold to breeders who want to eliminate odors from their catteries. Never clean a urine spot with ammonia because urine contains ammonia, and this might encourage your cat to continue using the same inappropriate place.

Urine Marking

Another form of territorial behavior in cats is urine marking, or spraying. Spraying is different from urinating outside the litterbox and can be identified by the posture cats assume while engaging in the activity. Urination is done from a squatting position onto a horizontal surface, although some cats begin to raise their posteriors as they eliminate, making high-sided litterboxes a necessity in some homes. Urine marking is accomplished from a standing position and the urine is sprayed onto a vertical surface such as a wall or piece of furniture. Urine marking primarily occurs among male cats, but female cats have been known to spray as well. Unneutered male cats (toms) routinely spray, especially during the spring and summer when females most often come into heat. Urine marks have a distinctly strong odor and can give a house a decidedly catty smell if not controlled or neutralized.

Neutering a male cat before it is sexually mature (about six to eight months old) will eliminate its desire to urine mark in most cases. Unless you have purchased a male Manx that is part of a breeding program, have it neutered before the marking behavior

A tailed Manx kitten and a Manx without a tail engage in play on the Isle of Man.

starts. Circumstances that develop outside or inside the home may prompt the behavior to occur occasionally, even among neutered males. Stressful situations such as the presence of intact males outside or overcrowding of cats inside may cause a cat to initiate such behaviors. Once the urine marking starts, it may continue unless you take steps either to eliminate the source of the problem or to modify the cat's behavior. Feliway, a commercial product that initiates feline exploratory behavior and eating in new situations (see page 34) also helps stop spraying among cats indoors. Spray it around the room on walls, furniture, and other objects at a height of about 18 inches. If intact males frequently roam outside your home, try to find their owners or contact an animal welfare organization and talk to them about neuter and release programs for feral cats.

If your Manx has sprayed in your house, clean with an effective odor neutralizer to

The presence of cats outside the home may cause an indoor cat to spray.

help prevent your cat from returning to the spot. Keep your Manx from entering the room it has marked or, because cats don't like to eat where they spray, change the function of the place to an eating location. If stress inside the home, such as the presence of a new cat, is causing your Manx to spray, separate the two animals and reintroduce them gradually. As a last resort, discuss drug therapy with your veterinarian. A prescription medication used to reduce anxiety in humans has been used to successfully treat spraying in cats.

Doing Their Nails

Cats, even domestic ones, are born hunters, and claws are an important part of their weaponry, so keeping them razor-sharp serves an important function. Cats remove the dead sheaths from their claws by scratching surfaces that include wood, carpet, sisal rope, and fabric. The scratched surface is also thought to be a visual marker to other cats, as well as a scent marker carrying deposits left by the cat's sebaceous glands as it claws. Cats, however, are seldom seen investigating objects clawed by other cats.

Research into feline behavior may find that scratching serves a purely practical purpose, but your cat will need to scratch something regardless of its motives. A scratch post that contains a variety of appealing surfaces will go a long way toward protecting your belongings from your Manx when it must do its nails. Protect the corners of your sofas and chairs by placing smaller posts in front of them, covering them with aluminum foil, spraying them with a product designed to keep cats away, or dabbing them with an oil that is offensive to your cat's olfactory system, such as citrus, eucalyptus, cinnamon, or clove. Test a piece of fabric first to make sure that it can withstand whatever oil you intend to use.

Training Your Manx

Cats have long had a reputation for being untrainable, but that myth is going the same way as the myths that say, "Cats need milk" and "Cats are solitary animals." Training your Manx to come when called will provide it an extra measure of safety if it should escape through an open door. Training your Manx to get down will prevent it from behaving in ways that may be unacceptable to you, such as jumping onto the dining room table, or will

protect it from hazards such as hot stove burners. Your Manx also can be trained to do tricks, such as sit up, fetch, or beg. Even if trick training is something you don't care to do, providing your Manx with consistent lessons that teach it the rules of the household will help prevent behavior problems from developing.

Training your Manx takes two forms: teaching it what to do and teaching it what not to do. You will have a greater rate of success if you use teaching methods that involve positive instead of negative reinforcement. Some schools of thought advise cat owners to booby trap a location to keep their cats from going there. The noise from empty aluminum cans, for example, falling off the kitchen counter is thought to discourage a cat from jumping on the counter again. Electric shock mats are intended to do the same. A squirt bottle aimed at the cat just when it is engaging in an inappropriate activity will discourage it from performing that activity again. While these techniques may have some success, they also have disadvantages. What cat owner wants stacks of aluminum cans sitting everywhere that is off-limits to their cats, which, when they fall, will frighten not only the cat but everyone else within earshot? Who wants to constantly carry a squirt gun to reprimand the cat every time it does something it shouldn't? And who wants to destroy the trust he or she has spent so much time building with the cat they've chosen to bring into their homes? Ask any professional animal trainer, whether they train domestic or wild cats, and you'll find that the method they use is a conditioned response technique that involves reward for right action rather than punishment for behaving incorrectly.

Positive Reinforcement

When you use your electric can opener or shake a container of catnip and your Manx comes running, conditioned response is already working in your home. Using conditioned response to train your Manx to obey commands is simply a continuation of what has been occurring naturally. In the process, you will be using rewards that your Manx will associate with the commands you are teaching. The most effective reward is food, but you also can use crumpled paper balls or other toys to reward your Manx for performing the command correctly. In time, you will discover that your Manx has trained *you* to feed it while you play!

If you are using food as a reward, conduct the training session before mealtime. Select a quiet place where you can conduct the session without distractions. Train for only 10 or 15 minutes at a time to prevent your Manx from tiring or becoming bored. Decide beforehand what words you will use for the commands and use them consistently. Teach only one command at a time. Repeat the lesson each day and, after it is learned, move on to the next command. When training, use your cat's name along with the command you are trying to teach. In addition to offering the reward, pet and praise your Manx when it performs the command you are teaching. You also can accustom your Manx to associating the command with a sound such as clucking with your tongue, snapping your fingers, or clicking a child's cricket, a small metal device that clicks when squeezed. Make the associative noise every time you give the command in each session. In time, you need only make the noise to initiate the response. Using something you always have with you, such as your fingers or tongue, will help in situations when the cricket device is not always handy.

Come: Give your Manx a piece of the food treat before beginning. Say your Manx's name and give the command, "Come." Hold out the food reward. When your Manx comes, offer it a piece of food and give it lots of praise. Repeat the process, backing up with each repetition. If your cat does not come, pause or postpone the session. As your Manx learns the command, praise it but do not offer it a reward each time. Gradually decrease the reward, offering it only some of the time. Eventually, your Manx will learn to come when it is called for the praise as much as for the reward.

Sit: Start when your Manx is standing. Say your Manx's name and give the command "Sit." With a food treat in your hand, move the food up and over your Manx's head toward its back to make it sit down. Make a clicking sound and say "Sit" again. If your Manx sits, praise it and offer a food reward. Repeat the process. If your Manx appears frustrated or impatient, save the lesson for another time. Continue the process until your cat begins to associate the command with the reward. You can use these same techniques to get your cat to learn other commands such as "Down," "Roll over," or "Stay."

Whatever you decide to train your cat to do or not to do, be patient and consistent. Your Manx will thank you by offering you its companionship and love for its entire life.

NUTRITION AND FEEDING

The Role of Good Nutrition

No one will deny that a good diet pays off in many ways. This is true for your Manx kitten or cat. Until a kitten reaches the age of six to eight weeks, its nutritional requirements are met by its mother. Once a kitten is weaned, it becomes the responsibility of its human caregiver to provide it with a diet to ensure that it grows into a healthy adult cat and to help it maintain optimal health throughout its life. Good nutrition will show in the condition of your cat's coat. Because a shiny, sleek coat is a sign of a healthy cat, your Manx's coat will play an important role in how it is judged if you compete in cat shows. Conversely, if your Manx is ill, one of the first signs will be poor coat condition. Good nutrition also will help keep your cat's energy level at its best, improve its resistance to infection and disease, and prevent it from developing disorders associated with an inadequate, incomplete, or inappropriate diet.

Building Blocks of Life

Like all animals, including the human, cats need specific nutrients to maintain their bodies' systems. Your Manx is no exception. Adequate amounts of protein, vitamins, minerals, fats, and water are fundamental to your Manx's health. Although the calculations for determining adequate levels can be quite complex, even for the experienced cat owner or breeder, suffice it to say that most manufacturers of pet foods have done their homework and formulated their products to meet the dietary needs of our feline companions (see pages 55–59).

Protein in your Manx's diet should come from a variety of sources such as meat, fowl, fish, organ meats, and by-products. Present in proteins are 22 amino acids that your Manx needs to produce muscle, skin, enzymes, and blood. Of those, only 10 are required in their diets. The remainder can be manufactured as part of the digestive process.

Vitamins: Cats need vitamins for growth and maintenance of body tissue and for metabolism of other nutrients. Both too little vitamin content in a cat's diet and too much of certain vitamins can cause health problems. Vitamins are either fat soluble, such as A, D, E, or K, or water soluble, such as B-complex and C. Water soluble vitamins not used immediately are passed from the cat's body as waste products. Fat soluble vitamins not used immediately during digestive processes are stored in the body's fat. As a result of potential toxicity from too much A and D, veterinarians recommend that you not give your cat vitamin supplements unless advised to do so.

Minerals aid in bone and teeth formation and growth, muscle and nerve function, prevention of anemia, cell oxygenation, and proper functioning of the thyroid gland. Minerals work in combination with one another, and like the other essential nutrients, are present in adequate quantities in good commercial cat foods.

Carbohydrates: Their role in cat food is still being questioned. Cats show no real need for the sugars and starches that make up dietary carbohydrates.

Fats provide cats with adequate energy. Dietary fatty acids help maintain good coats and prevent liver problems.

Water: Cats require water to facilitate their body processes. Water makes up more than 70 percent of a cat's body. Your Manx will obtain some of its water from its food, especially canned food, which contains up to 78 percent water. Too much water intake as well as too little can signal a health problem, such as hyperthyroidism, kidney disease, high fever, or feline lower urinary tract disease, so monitor the water your Manx consumes, especially as it ages. Provide your Manx with fresh water every day. Some cats prefer to drink at locations away from their food bowls, so try placing water bowls at various locations throughout the house for easy access. Manx have a reputation for playing in their water as well as drinking it, so you may find your Manx dipping more than its mouth in the dish, using its water bowl for entertainment as well as wetting its whiskers.

Cats Are Carnivores

Occasionally, well-meaning cat owners who have sought more humane lifestyles for themselves by becoming vegetarians have tried to impose those values onto their cats. Although dogs can derive their proteins from some vegetables, those sources just don't cut it with *felis catus*. Millions of years of evolution have produced an animal designed to require animal sources for its protein utilization. Unlike animals that can manufacture some of the amino acids they require during the digestive process, the cat requires dietary sources that contain meat protein. The essential amino acid taurine is one that cats can't manufacture, and must be obtained from meat sources in the cat's diet. Lack of taurine can lead to vision problems and contribute to cardiomyopathy. Cats consuming inadequate amounts of taurine may not reproduce normally. Many animals can derive vitamin A, an essential nutrient for good vision and skin metabolism, from

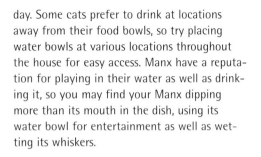

Manx enjoy playing with their water as well as drinking it.

beta carotene found in plant foods such as carrots. To be of use by the feline digestive process, however, the vitamin A must come from meat sources rather than vegetable ones. Most animals can manufacture the essential fatty acid called arachidomic acid from supplies of linoleic acid found in vegetable sources. The cat, unable to manufacture its own arachidomic acid, must obtain it directly from meat. If you consider a vegetarian diet necessary for a pet you bring into your home, consider adopting a dog or goldfish rather than a cat. Imposing vegetarianism on your cat will do it more harm than good.

The Right Foodstuff

Cats have a reputation for being finicky eaters, but today's pet food manufacturers have developed enough types of food products and flavors to satisfy even the most discriminating feline taste buds. Cat food comes in three basic types along with a myriad of treats, milk substitutes, and tartar control items for occasional use.

Wet or canned food is a favorite among many cats. Although it is more expensive than the other two types of food, it is generally more palatable, and your Manx may prefer it. Wet food can contain more than 70 percent water, and is a good dietary source of that essential nutrient. Canned food comes in 2.5-ounce (70.8-g) sizes all the way up to the large 14-ounce (397-g) cans, which are less expensive on an ounce-per-ounce basis. If you have only one or two cats, the large cans are enough for several meals, but uneaten portions must be refrigerated to maintain freshness. You may find your Manx turning its nose up at food that has been refrigerated, so

warming it up to room temperature in the microwave may make it more tempting. Check with a finger to be sure it is not hot before serving your Manx.

Semimoist cat food was developed more as a convenience to cat owners than as a good food for cats. Its longer shelf life and moist texture are maintained by preservatives that prevent spoilage. Semimoist cat food hardens relatively quickly after exposure to the air, making it less palatable to cats.

Dry cat food is the most economical. Because it contains less water than wet food, cats eat less of it. Dry food doesn't attract insects or spoil quickly, so it can be free-fed to a cat. Chewing dry food also helps keep your Manx's teeth clean.

Human food is not formulated for cats' dietary needs, so feeding your Manx what you are having for dinner may result in health problems. If you have a concern about preservatives or artificial coloring added to pet food and would like to cook for your Manx so that you have complete control over what it eats, obtain a book containing recipes that have been formulated to provide all the nutrients your Manx requires. You may feed table scraps occasionally, but keep the quantity under 10 percent of your Manx's total diet.

Fat Cat

How much you feed your cat depends on the type of food and the size, age, and weight of your cat. To avoid becoming too thin or too fat, a cat should take in the same amount of calories it expends. Counting calories can be an impossible task, so a good rule of thumb is to feel your cat's side. Every cat has a layer of subcutaneous fat, but you should be able to feel its rib cage beneath the skin. A cat should not be so thin that its bones show nor so fat that you cannot feel its ribs, and its diet should help maintain that condition. Manufacturers suggest quantities on their packages, but in most cases the suggested amounts are more than your cat will need, especially if your cat's meals contain wet and dry. If you are uncertain, discuss it with your veterinarian or ask the breeder how much your Manx was fed before you purchased it. The breeder from whom you obtained your Manx will be able to tell you what types and brands of food the cat was fed at the cattery. If you want to change your Manx's diet, do it gradually over a period of 7 to 10 days by providing some of the new food as well as some of its previous diet. Sudden changes in a cat's feeding regimen can result in digestive problems or unwillingness to eat. Ideally, a cat should be fed twice a day at scheduled times, although what is fed at each meal can vary. Contrary to the popular notion, a cat will not necessarily eat

if it gets hungry enough, so leaving the dish of food on the floor is no guarantee your cat eventually will eat it. If your cat refuses to eat for more than a day, a trip to the veterinarian is in order. If a cat goes without eating for more than 48 hours, its liver can begin to shut down. So, if your new Manx decides to go on a hunger strike, be willing to experiment with new foods and flavors to get it eating again.

Once a kitten is weaned, it no longer has a need for milk. Milk contains lactose, and if your Manx cannot break down the lactose in the intestinal wall, the presence of lactose can produce diarrhea. If you would like to give your cat milk occasionally, purchase a commercially available milk substitute in the pet food section of the supermarket.

Regardless of the type of food you decide to feed your cat, variety is important to prevent it from relying on a food that may not be nutritionally complete. If you ever must feed your cat a special diet to solve or manage a health problem, you shouldn't have trouble getting your cat to eat the new food if it was accustomed to eating different flavors and types of food all its life. Protein should come from sources that include meat, poultry, and fish to avoid deficiencies that might develop from consuming food from only one source such as organ meats.

Warning: Although your cat might like tuna, because of its higher magnesium and inadequate

Good nutrition will be reflected in the condition of your cat's coat.

nutritional content for cats, tuna is a food that is best left on the supermarket shelf or offered only in tiny quantities as an occasional treat.

A balanced diet helps ensure a long life of companionship.

Premium vs. Commercial

In addition to good commercial food that can be found in your local supermarket, premium food is available for pet owners at pet supply stores or through veterinarians. Although premium is considerably more expensive than other commercial foods, manufacturers justify the higher prices by consistently using the same ingredients rather than varying ingredients according to what is available at the time. There is no conclusive evidence, however, that premium foods are better than commercial ones or that cats fed premium diets live longer or are healthier than those that do not.

Life Stages

Pet food manufacturers produce foods formulated to meet the needs of cats in all stages of their lives, from kittenhood through old age. Because nutritional and caloric requirements change as a cat ages, the various foods have different quantities of certain nutrients. Kittens can have more than a 2,000 percent increase over their birth weight during the first 20 weeks of life. Research has shown that growing kittens, therefore, need greater concentrations of protein, vitamins A and D, fatty acids, and minerals such as calcium, phosphorous, and magnesium. As your cat passes through adulthood to life as a senior, its caloric intake lowers because its activity level decreases, and its food requirements change again.

As your cat ages, it may lose teeth and experience degenerative diseases. Feeding a special diet may help you manage your cat's illness and symptoms. Foods formulated for the needs of seniors are commercially available. Although most manufacturers consider a 7-year-old cat to be senior, the 14-year average life span may make that a little soon to be putting a cat in that category.

Deciphering Cat Food Labels

A lot of information is packed onto cat food labels, and reading their tiny print, never mind understanding what the information means, can take time and effort. The good news is that cat food labeling must follow a standard that has been developed by the Association of American Feed Control Officials (AAFCO), which determines not only what goes on a label but the sequence in which it appears. Reading the label is the best way to determine whether the food meets the stringent AAFCO testing standards developed to provide your cat with optimum nutrition. Cat food that has been formulated according to AAFCO guidelines and is complete and nutritionally balanced will have a guarantee that reads, "Animal feeding tests using AAFCO procedures substantiate that (brand name) provides complete and balanced nutrition for (life stage of) cats."

The information panel will tell you what is in the food. It begins with the guaranteed analysis section, which contains the sources for ingredients listed in the order of their percentages of total content from highest to lowest. It tells the consumer the minimum amounts of protein and fat and the maximum amounts of fiber and water contained in the product. Crude protein, crude fat, crude fiber, and moisture are listed in decreasing percentages. The term crude refers to the method used to estimate the quantity of that ingredient in food, and is based on nitrogen contained in the product. Cat food labels also must contain the mineral content such as calcium, salt, phosphorus, taurine, and ash, which is the noncombustible material left in the food after processing.

The ingredients are listed after the guaranteed analysis. Ingredients are listed in order of highest to lowest quantity by weight. If the label says *meat,* it will be from the clean flesh, or muscle, of the animal. Meat can also include tissue from the tongue, diaphragm, heart, and esophagus. *Meat-by-products* are the nonrendered clean parts other than meat, including blood, brains, stomach, intestines, and other organs, but not hair, hooves, bones, or ears. *Meat meal* is ground into powder and contains renderings from the processing plant. These can include whatever the plant has at the time. If the by-product has bone in it, the label must say *meat and bone meal.*

Poultry by-products are the leftover parts of the chicken or turkey that humans don't eat. This can include heads, feet, and viscera. *Poultry meal* contains the flesh and skin with or without bone that, like meat meal, is ground into a powder. If a cat food label says chicken or chicken by-products, it must be chicken and not turkey or *vice versa.* Fish and fish meal are used in the same way. Fish oil is often added to enhance flavor.

Ground corn, wheat flour, rice, or soy are added as fillers or to add fiber to the food and may not be nutritionally required. Manufacturers may add vitamins, minerals, fats, and amino acids such as taurine to their products. Other additives enhance the color, flavor, and aroma and are intended to either make the food more palatable to pets or more visually appealing to pet owners. Any artificial color or flavor that is added to pet food must be approved by the U.S. Department of Agriculture (USDA). Many manufacturers are eliminating artificial colors because of concern over consumer perception of potential health problems.

Antioxidants that are added to food to preserve its shelf life and prevent spoilage appear on the label. Natural antioxidants include vitamins E and C. Other preservatives can include synthetic antioxidants such as butylated hydroxyanisole (BHA) and butylated hydroxytoluene (BHT). The label also states if artificial color has been added.

Dietary Disorders

Obesity

Cats can develop problems associated with their diets that may be related to type of food, quantity, or source. Cats that take in more calories than they expend may become overweight and lethargic. As with their human companions, obesity is the number one food related problem in pets, and once the excess pounds appear, it is more difficult to take them off than it is to prevent them in the first place. If your Manx is to lose weight, it must increase its activity level, reduce its caloric intake, or both. Light-formula cat foods help a cat lower its caloric intake, but regular exercise will have the added benefit of helping to keep your cat

fit, trim, and longer-lived. Keeping your cat active and controlling its food consumption are the best ways to prevent obesity.

Allergies

Cats occasionally develop allergies to certain foods or the additives in foods. If your Manx develops a skin rash, excessive itching, or loss of hair, and you suspect it has developed a food allergy, you can treat it by putting the cat on a eight-week, hypoallergenic diet recommended by your veterinarian. If the problem disappears, you can gradually add various foods to its menu plan until the symptoms reappear, at which time you will have identified the culprit and can eliminate it permanently from your cat's diet.

Feline Lower Urinary Tract Disease

A major diet-related problem is feline lower urinary tract disease (FLUTD), a condition that arises when crystals form in a cat's bladder and block the passage of urine. Urinary tract blockage can be life threatening if not caught in time. Cats with FLUTD may appear to strain when trying to eliminate, urinate more often than usual, pass only small amounts of liquid wastes, pass blood in their urine, or urinate in unusual places. Foods that have a lower alkaline pH and are lower in magnesium content help control FLUTD. Cats prone to FLUTD should have adequate amounts of fresh water to help encourage the flow of wastes through their lower digestive tract. If you suspect your Manx has developed FLUTD, take it to your veterinarian immediately. Discuss with him or her feeding options to help control the problem.

HEALTH CARE FOR YOUR MANX

The Great Indoors

Cats are living an average of 14 years, thanks to advances in feline medicine and nutrition as well as improvements in their lifestyles. By providing your Manx with proper health care and a safe environment, you can expect to share its love and companionship for a long time. When you obtain your Manx from a reputable breeder, he or she may give you a health guarantee that, based on the quality care already provided, your kitten should grow up to be a sturdy, healthy cat.

One of the important ways you can help protect your Manx from succumbing to accidents or contracting infectious diseases is to keep it indoors. The indoor lifestyle will prevent your Manx from coming into contact with cats and other animals whose health status is unknown. While most contagious diseases that pose a problem to your Manx are passed from cat to cat, still others, such as rabies, can be passed between species. Your Manx, if allowed to go outside unattended, can fall victim to not only contagious diseases but also harmful accidents, poisons, parasites, and the vicious deeds of inhumane people.

While it's true that your Manx cat's physical health will benefit from the vitamin D present in sunlight, it will receive adequate amounts of it from a nutritionally balanced diet. If you would like your Manx to benefit emotionally from basking in the sun's warm glow, you can encourage it to lie at open, screened windows, give it restricted access to the outdoors with an enclosed run, or allow it supervised outdoor playtime on a harness and leash.

Although keeping your Manx indoors is safer and kinder than allowing it to roam, it's not a complete guarantee that it will be 100 percent free of illness or injury. You also put your Manx at risk by not providing regular medical care, by not creating a safe environment, or by introducing other cats into your home without first having them examined and tested for contagious diseases such as feline leukemia (FLV) or feline immunodeficiency virus (FIV), among others. To help keep your indoor Manx healthy and physically sound, you will need to provide additional veterinary attention for him.

Veterinary Care

Annual Checkups

Purchasing a Manx from a reputable breeder will go a long way in ensuring the health of your cat, but annual veterinary checkups will contribute to the overall well-being of your

Manx and add to the quality of its life. A veterinarian will detect any problems or diseases early and recommend treatment to prevent their spread. He or she will weigh your Manx, examine its eyes, ears and mouth, and check your Manx's teeth and gums. He will palpate the kidneys to assess whether they are enlarged or shrunken, feel its bladder size for buildup of fluids that might denote a urinary tract blockage, check for lumps or bumps on or under the skin, look for signs of external parasites, and, if symptoms require or you request it, do a blood workup to detect the presence of diseases. He will perform a fecal examination of a stool sample you provide to detect internal parasites.

Vaccinating Your Manx

One of the first precautions you should take with your new Manx kitten is to have it vaccinated if it hasn't already been vaccinated by the breeder. Kittens depend on their mothers for a lot of things. Anyone who has had to change a baby's diapers will no doubt think that urinating and defecating are bodily functions that come naturally. Newborn kittens, however, will not initiate the processes until their mother licks their anal area. Kittens also obtain a certain degree of immunization through drinking their mother's milk. As the kitten is weaned at six to eight weeks of age, the natural immunity will fade, requiring help in the form of vaccinations to continue the immune process.

A vaccination is the administration of a vaccine that contains the presence of foreign antigens intended to stimulate the body to produce a natural immune response to fight off a particular disease. When vaccinated, your Manx's immune system will generate specialized pro-

teins, called antibodies, that will help it develop resistance to bacteria, viruses, or toxins. This process is called immunization. By virtue of having been exposed to the particular disease antigens, your Manx's immune system will continue to fight off the offending contagions when it comes into contact with them. Because immunity can decrease over time, it is necessary to periodically boost your Manx cat's immunity to specific diseases by having your veterinarian re-vaccinate it or give it booster shots.

Inactivated or killed vaccines are the safest type because the infectious agent present in the vaccine will not replicate in the body or cause the disease to which the agent is meant to trigger immunity. Killed vaccines tend to take longer to become effective and produce a shorter immune response.

Modified live vaccines contain viruses that have been chemically altered so that they do not produce the disease in question, but retain their ability to replicate in the vaccinated animal. Modified live vaccines produce the most rapid, long-lasting immune response, but, while it is taking effect, there is a small chance the virus can be shed from the vaccinated cat to other cats with whom he comes into contact and infect either the vaccinated pet or other animals with the disease it was meant to protect against.

Reduce Risk of Disease

A veterinarian will administer vaccines intramuscularly, subcutaneously, or intranasally depending on the instructions from the vaccine's manufacturer. The series of shots will vary slightly from veterinarian to veterinarian, but the series can begin as early as six weeks of age. Kittens aged 6 to 12 weeks should be given a three-way series of shots called FVRCP-feline viral rhinotracheitis, calicivirus, and panleukopenia. The shots are given in a series of two to three shots at three-week intervals, starting at the age of 6 to 8 weeks for healthy kittens, and 12 to 15 weeks for kittens whose development might be delayed.

The FVR and FCV parts of the vaccine are to help your cat fight off feline viral rhinotracheitis and feline calicivirus, common and contagious respiratory diseases. Respiratory viruses pose a serious threat because the viruses causing the disease live outside the body of the animal for several hours to several days, and therefore can be transmitted without direct contact with an infected cat.

Feline viral rhinotracheitis (FVR) and feline calicivirus (FCV) account for the majority of feline respiratory diseases. Signs of the disease include sneezing, coughing, nasal discharge, and watery eyes. An infected cat can become dehydrated and lose its appetite. The virus is transmitted through an infected cat's saliva, nasal and ocular discharges, feces, and urine, depending on which virus is the culprit. Spread of the disease is through direct contact with infected cats or by contact with contaminated cages, food and water dishes, bedding, and litterboxes. Even cats kept indoors can contract the disease through open windows or, if you have touched an infected cat, transmission on your hands and clothing. Cats in crowded conditions with other cats may contract the disease from infected cats. Keep your Manx's vaccinations up to date for your cat's sake and the sake of other cats.

The third component of the vaccine is intended to strengthen a cat's immune system against feline panleukopenia (FP) or, as it's commonly called, feline distemper—a highly contagious viral disease characterized by fever, loss of appetite, dehydration, vomiting, and a decrease in white blood cells. Transmission of feline panleukopenia virus can occur through direct contact with an infected cat, contaminated living quarters or objects such as food bowls, litter pans or bedding, or the hands or clothing of someone who has touched an infected cat. The mortality rate for feline panleukopenia is high, and kittens, as a result of their undeveloped immune systems, are most susceptible to contracting it.

Boosters

If you have purchased your Manx from a reputable breeder, the kitten's health will have been established as sound before you purchased it. By the age of 16 weeks, when most breeders allow purchase of their kittens, your Manx most likely will have been given the vaccinations necessary to protect its health. If the kitten vaccination series is completed by the time you purchase your Manx, discuss with your veterinarian if and when boosters will be necessary to help it continue to fight contagious diseases. Verify what vaccinations were given to your Manx at the time you purchased it.

If your Manx kitten has not been vaccinated, or if you have obtained your kitten from a source other than an established breeder, and it has not been immunized or its immunization status is unknown, check with your veterinarian about obtaining the proper vaccinations to help ensure your kitten's health.

The Older Cat

If you are purchasing an older Manx, request a copy of the cat's medical records, which should include its vaccination schedule and any other

Cats allowed to roam outside are at risk from contagious diseases, accidents, parasites, and other potentially harmful situations.

health-related issues. Provide the records to your own veterinarian to help him or her give your Manx continued quality care and to prevent duplication of tests or vaccinations that already may have been given.

Vaccination Controversy

A controversial issue in the veterinary community is the topic of vaccination site sarcomas—malignant tumors that can develop at the location on the animal where a vaccination was administered. Chemical additives, called adjuvants—most notably aluminum salts—which make a killed vaccine work more quickly, are what researchers initially felt might con-

tribute to the cause of this malady. Some of the currently available vaccines have adjuvants other than aluminum, and some are without adjuvants. Although it is felt that adjuvants play some role in the development of these tumors, they are not the sole culprits, because it has been shown that vaccines with other adjuvants or with no adjuvants can result in tumor formation.

Although the incidence of vaccination site sarcomas has been found to be only one in ten thousand (.01 percent) to one in one thousand (.1 percent) of all cats receiving vaccinations, veterinary studies done in 1991–92 by Dr. Mattie Hendrick, a veterinarian at the University of Pennsylvania, have shown that the incidence of vaccination site sarcomas is on the rise. Cat owners can minimize the risk by making sure that their veterinarians are aware of the potential problem and vaccinate using proper vaccination protocols. Although no one brand of vaccine has been identified as causing the sarcomas, veterinarians and breeders should keep records of vaccine manufacturers, lot numbers, vaccination sites, and any adverse reactions, and report their findings to the Adverse Drug Experiences Reporting Division, USDA (see Information for the address from which your veterinarian can obtain a reporting form, page 100). A March 1998 report in the journal *Veterinary Medicine* indicates that unnecessary vaccinations may place the feline patient at risk and impart financial and emotional hardship on the owner. Unnecessary vaccinations are those for diseases that don't affect a large percentage of the feline population or those not associated with high mortality rates. As examples, the article cites vaccines for Lyme disease, ringworm, feline infectious peritonitis (FIP), and, for indoors-only cats, feline leukemia virus (FeLV). Most vaccines are considered safe and effective, however. Of the millions of cats vaccinated against contagious diseases every year, only a small number develop vaccination site sarcomas. The threat of certain diseases is far greater than the threat of sarcomas developing as a result of vaccinations, so advising cat owners not to vaccinate their cats because of the threat of sarcoma is like advising them not to wear seat belts because a small portion of accident victims would have been better off had they not been wearing them. Discuss with your veterinarian the appropriateness of vaccinating your cat.

Other Contagious Diseases

Your Manx kitten should be free of contagious diseases at the time of purchase. Reputable Manx breeders routinely test their cats for contagious diseases to prevent them from accidentally spreading the disease to other cats in a cattery or from parent cats to their offspring.

Feline leukemia virus impairs a cat's immune system, making the cat unable to fight off the effects of the virus and susceptible to other illnesses as well. Infected cats secrete the virus and are a source of infection for all healthy cats with which they come into contact. The FeLV virus is transmitted primarily through saliva, respiratory secretions, urine, and feces. Social grooming and licking and

sharing litterboxes, food dishes, and water bowls are ways the leukemia virus is transmitted from one cat to another. Feline leukemia also can be transmitted *in utero* or through milk from a mother to her offspring.

FeLV produces different symptoms in different cats and is often difficult to detect until the cat is tested for the disease. Poor coat, loss of weight, lethargy, anorexia, and stunted growth are common symptoms. Cats with leukemia can develop kidney disease, reproductive disorders, anemia, tumors, and neurological problems and can lose their blood-clotting ability. A large portion of cats that have chronic infections of the mouth and gum, abscesses, skin and ear infections, or feline infectious peritonitis are suspected of having feline leukemia virus.

Nearly one third of cats exposed to feline leukemia virus develop a natural immunity to the disease and never become ill. The remainder may become latent carriers but never succumb to the effects of the disease. A latent carrier poses a threat to other cats in some circumstances. If the cat becomes stressed, for example, or develops another disease, the virus may reemerge, causing the clinical feline leukemia. A queen who bears a litter of kittens may pass the virus on to her offspring. The remaining cats that persistently test positive for FeLV die from the effects of the leukemia within three years of contracting the virus. If your Manx tests positive for feline leukemia, have him retested within three to four weeks.

The feline leukemia virus is chemically unstable and lives for only a few minutes outside the body. It can be destroyed by common household detergents and alcohol, so washing bedding, bowls, and litterboxes will enable a new cat to enter a household once inhabited by a leukemia-positive cat almost immediately.

There is no cure for feline leukemia. Cats suspected of having the disease should be tested. Any cats brought into a household containing other cats should be tested before allowing them to join in the communal living environment. Cats testing negative can be vaccinated against the disease. Your veterinarian can advise you on whether to vaccinate and what commercial vaccine to use. Cats kept indoors are less likely to come into contact with feline leukemia.

FIP is a deadly disease that is difficult to diagnose and, as with feline leukemia, has no cure. A veterinarian will use a combination of clinical symptoms and laboratory tests to determine if a cat has the disease. Laboratory tests can detect the presence of antibodies to coronaviruses, of which FIP is one, but cannot specifically identify the FIP virus. A new test called polymerase chain reaction (PCR) is being marketed by some laboratories. It is thought to be more accurate in identifying the strains of the coronavirus causing FIP, but it will only tell if the cat has been exposed and has mounted an antibody response as a result of the exposure, but cannot determine if the cat is infected with FIP.

There are two types of FIP—wet and dry—which are determined by fluid accumulation, particularly in the abdominal cavity, that causes enlargement of the abdomen. Cats with the wet type of FIP will look extremely bloated from the shoulders down. If the fluid occurs in the chest cavity, respiratory problems may occur. Other signs of FIP are nonspecific and include fever, loss of appetite, weight loss, and depression.

Fortunately, FIP is fairly uncommon, even in catteries and households with many cats.

Most cats that contract FIP also have other immune-suppressing conditions such as feline leukemia. A vaccine to prevent FIP is on the market, but much controversy surrounds its use. In FIP, antibodies actually contribute to its clinical severity, and since the FIP vaccine stimulates an antibody response, it may not be protective. Also, the vaccine could cause the cat to become sicker if it is exposed to FIP than it would have had it not been vaccinated at all. The effectiveness of the vaccine is still undetermined.

Feline immunodeficiency virus (FIV), commonly called "feline AIDS," is another immune-suppressing virus for which there is no cure. Although the virus is in the same subfamily as those that cause similar problems in other species—including HIV, which affects humans—it is not related, nor can it be passed from cat to person and *vice versa*.

Transmission of FIV is uncertain but thought to be through bite wounds from infected cats. Symptoms of FIV are diverse and difficult to pinpoint because of a host of secondary infections, anemia, and low white blood cell count. Mouth and teeth problems such as gingivitis (infection of the gums), stomatitis (infection of the mouth), and periodontis (inflamation of the tissue surrounding the teeth) are common signs of feline immunodeficiency virus. These secondary infections can lead to loss of appetite and eventual loss of the cat's teeth.

There is an FIV antibody test that will confirm the presence of the disease. No cure or vaccine for FIV exists. Cats kept indoors and away from free-roaming cats are unlikely to contract FIV.

Rabies is caused by a virus that attacks the central nervous system of warm-blooded animals. It is one of the few diseases that can be transmitted between different species. Your Manx can get rabies from the bite of a rabid animal or through infected saliva entering the body through an open wound, the eyes, or the mouth. The end result of rabies infection is death.

Rabies can be prevented by vaccination and by keeping your Manx indoors. Some states have laws requiring that pets be vaccinated against rabies. Your Manx kitten should be vaccinated for rabies after it reaches the age of 12 weeks, then receive a booster every one to three years thereafter, depending on state regulations and type of vaccine.

External Parasites

Fleas are the most common external parasite to inflict cats. Fleas are tiny but visible. If your Manx has fleas, however, you'll probably see the results of the flea infestation rather than the fleas themselves. Tiny specks resembling black pepper will be visible in your cat's coat and, if the infestation is a severe one, on anything upon which your cat has decided to sit or take a nap. The specks are bits of flea feces, eggs, and undigested blood that the flea deposits after biting your cat.

Even an indoor cat can get fleas, which can be carried in from the yard on your clothing and other pets. Fleas lay eggs most actively when the temperatures are above 65°F (33°C) and the humidity is above 75 percent, making an infestation especially devastating in warm climates or during the summer months. As a result of bites, some cats may develop an allergic response resulting in itchy, reddened, or crusty patches on the skin, typically on the lower back and base of the tail, the inner thighs, the head, and the neck.

Keeping your Manx indoors will lessen the likelihood of its contracting fleas, but there is no guarantee. There are several ways to keep your Manx from getting fleas. A commercial product given internally in pill or liquid form or through a six-month shot, is administered in one-month or six-month doses. It works by damaging the flea eggs, thus breaking the flea's life cycle. Topical products that are applied directly to your cat's coat break the flea cycle by killing adult fleas before they have a chance to lay eggs. Once treated, the fleas die upon contact with your cat's skin or hair. You apply a monthly premeasured dose that spreads on the surface of your cat's skin at the hair root to provide whole-body coverage. One treatment kills fleas for a month. Other flea products include sprays, powders, dips, shampoos, soap, roll-ons, mousses, herbals, flea collars, and disposable dampened topical cloths.

If you are using any of these products on your cat, you must get rid of the fleas, eggs, and larvae in your home as well. Foggers, misters, flea trays, or premise sprays help remove the pests from floors, bedding, carpet, and furniture.

Some flea products work by using natural ingredients, while others rely on chemicals. *To avoid accidental poisoning, never combine flea products on your Manx and never use products intended for dogs.* Discuss with your veterinarian the options for getting rid of the fleas, then follow the package directions.

Ear mites: If you see your Manx shaking its head, scratching its ears, or engaging in restless behavior, or you notice a brown substance in its ears, chances are it has ear mites—microscopic parasites that live in a cat's ears. Kittens may contract ear mites from their mothers, although adult cats can contract them from

Symptoms of Illness in Your Manx
- ◆ Blood in stools or urine
- ◆ Coughing or sneezing
- ◆ Crying for no apparent reason
- ◆ Diarrhea for more than 24 hours
- ◆ Gagging or retching
- ◆ Loss of hair
- ◆ Limping
- ◆ Discharge from nose or eyes
- ◆ Excessive scratching
- ◆ Tearing or cloudiness in eye
- ◆ Vomiting
- ◆ Wheezing
- ◆ Sleeping more than usual
- ◆ Eating less or refusing food
- ◆ Weight loss, even though eating normally
- ◆ Loss of interest in toys
- ◆ Drinking more water than usual
- ◆ Using the litterbox excessively
- ◆ Straining to urinate or defecate
- ◆ Exhibiting agressive or antisocial behavior

other sources as well, including infected dogs. Ear mites can be treated with medication.

Ticks are not a common problem in cats, but they can attach to your cat, especially if you allow it to go outside. Ticks are difficult to detect but appear as a tiny bump on the skin. A disease that is fatal to cats, *Cytauxzoon felis*, is carried by the dog tick. Ticks can be removed using a pair of tweezers, but be careful not to leave any mouth parts imbedded in your cat's skin. Ticks are the carriers of many diseases that also infect humans. If people live in an area endemic for tick-borne diseases, they must be careful, whether they have pets or not. Care must be taken when removing a tick from your cat. If it has engorged on your cat, it will not be able to follow up with a tasty meal of human blood, but

if it is not imbedded in your cat, it could attach itself to you. Although it is technically possible for humans to contract a tick-borne disease from a tick their cats have brought into the house, there is no evidence that people are at risk from contracting tick-borne diseases from their companion cats. Even dogs, which are more likely to bring ticks into the house after their daily walks, rarely pass them to people. Dog owners are likely to get ticks because they walk in the same places their dogs do.

Lyme disease is carried by the deer tick, and possibly by other ticks as well. Although cats have been infected by Lyme disease under experimental conditions, there have been no confirmed cases of cats clinically ill with Lyme disease. A vaccine exists to inoculate dogs against Lyme, but the vaccine has not been approved for cats.

Internal Parasites

Tapeworms can result when your cat ingests fleas or chooses an infected rodent for its daily meal, both of which act as intermediate hosts for the tapeworm. If you find fleas, you probably will discover tapeworms when segments, resembling rice or sesame seeds, leave your cat's body. Tapeworms can be treated easily, but to prevent them from recurring you must rid your cat and house of the fleas. Left untreated, tapeworms can rob your cat of nutrients, weaken its immune system, and leave it susceptible to other ailments.

Roundworms live in a cat's small intestines and can grow from 3 to 5 inches (7.6 to 12.7 cm) long. Roundworms are contagious, and cats can contract roundworms by ingesting the eggs in contaminated areas. A queen also can transmit roundworms to her kittens through her milk. Cats can pass the eggs in their stools unnoticed or regurgitate the adult worms, which resemble strings of spaghetti. The presence of roundworms is not life threatening unless the infestation is heavy, in which case intestinal blockage can result in death. A fecal exam conducted by your veterinarian will detect their presence. They can be treated with medication.

Signs of Illness

You can help keep your Manx healthy by closely observing it and by providing information to your veterinarian. In addition to your cat's annual checkup, home health exams will help you keep up with your cat's physical and emotional well-being.

Feline First Aid

Accidents or other severe problems will require that you administer first aid immediately before taking your Manx to the veterinarian or emergency clinic. First and foremost in any emergency: Remain calm. Keep your veterinarian's phone number and the number of an emergency clinic for off-hours problems handy so they are available if and when you should need them. If you suspect your Manx has ingested a poisonous substance, and you cannot reach your veterinarian, contact the The ASPCA National Animal Poison Control Center emergency hotline, which provides 24-hour-a-day, 7-day-a-week telephone assistance. The Center's hotline veterinarians can quickly answer questions about toxic chemicals, dangerous plants, products, or substances and assist in immediate treatment. When you call the ASPCA/NAPCC, be ready to provide

your name, address, telephone number, information concerning the exposure, age, sex, and weight of your Manx. In order to maintain operations, there is a fee for ASPCA/NAPCC services. The charge depends on which option you choose. Call 1-800-548-2423 or 1-888-4ANIHELP (1-888-426-4435), and you will be charged $30 per case including follow-ups. You must use Visa, MasterCard, Discover or American Express. If you call 1-900-680-0000, charges will appear on your phone bill. The cost is $20 for the first 5 minutes and $2.95 for each additional minute with a $20 minimum and no follow-ups.

Familiarize yourself with basic first aid techniques by purchasing a book on the topic. There are several good ones on the market. The American Red Cross and The Humane Society of the United States combined resources to produce a first aid manual, *The Pet First Aid Book*, which ties in with a first aid course being developed by the American Red Cross. In addition to a first aid manual, keep a kit handy for emergencies (see table).

First Aid Kit
- Blunt-tipped scissors for cutting bandages
- Flat end tweezers for removing ticks and sharp objects
- Rolls of gauze bandages in assorted thicknesses
- Cotton balls or cotton swabs
- 3 percent hydrogen peroxide for cleaning superficial cuts and abrasions
- Milk of magnesia and activated charcoal tablets for treatment of poisoning, with advice of veterinarian
- Antibacterial ointment

When your Manx is ill and needs to get something in its mouth, that's the time it may be the most resistant to opening it. Giving pills or liquid medications is a constant source of frustration to many cat owners, not to mention to cats, and the process tests the owners' ingenuity and patience.

Medication can be obtained from your veterinarian in liquid or pill form, and you may find your Manx prefers one over the other, which makes it easier to administer one type of medicine. Not all medications come in different forms, however, so you may not always have a choice, and knowing how to administer both types of medicine may turn out to be a necessity.

The Method

To administer medication in either liquid or pill form, kneel on the floor and place your Manx between your knees. If kneeling is difficult, place your Manx on a high surface such as a table or counter top. Place one hand around the top of your cat's head and lift backwards until your Manx opens its mouth. An extra pair of hands often makes it easier to restrain a cat while medicating, so if you have someone at home to help you, be sure to enlist assistance to help hold your Manx in case a getaway is foremost on its mind.

To give liquid medicine, insert the dropper inside your Manx's mouth and squirt all the liquid into its mouth.

Hold your Manx gently but firmly between your knees and tilt its head back until it opens its mouth.

If you are administering a pill, push the pill into the back of your Manx's throat and quickly close its mouth, holding it shut until you see your Manx swallow. If you prefer, use a pilling gun instead of your fingers to insert the pill. Pillers are available in pet stores or from your veterinarian. A pill gun is easy to use. Simply place the pill in the gun's rubber tip, insert it into your Manx's mouth. With your thumb, shoot the pill into the back of the mouth. Hold the mouth closed until you see your cat swallow.

Try hiding your cat's medicine in juice from its cat food can or in a bit of tasty meat.

Wrap your cat in a towel to protect yourself from painful scratches.

(top) Push the pill to the back of the cat's mouth, then hold its mouth shut until it swallows. (bottom) Insert the dropper between the last two teeth and squirt liquid medication into the mouth.

Preventing Injury

When pilling a cat, the greatest threat to the cat owner is from the cat's claws. In an attempt to resist your ministrations, your Manx may flail and claw at you, inflicting a painful injury. Keeping your cat's claws out of the way is important in the medicating procedure. If your Manx is especially uncooperative, wrap it in a towel to keep it from clawing you during the process. Another option is to wrap your Manx in a pillow case with only its head showing before you attempt the dread deed. A device that has come onto the market in recent years is an actual kitty straitjacket that restrains a cat's legs, preventing it from using its claws as weapons.

If all else fails, deception may be the best way to get medicine into the mouth of a resistant cat. Liquid medication can be disguised in some type of palatable food or treat, such as water from a can of tuna. A pill can be concealed inside a moist treat, a drop of butter, or baby food, or ground up with your Manx's dinner.

After you have successfully medicated your cat, spend some time with it and offer a treat to make the experience a pleasant one.

GOOD GROOMING

Why Bother?

Because most cats seem to spend most of their time preening, you may wonder why you have to contribute to the effort. But grooming serves a variety of functions, not just cleanliness. By washing its kittens, a mother cat establishes a close bond with them in the way a human mother bonds with a child through touch. Unless a kitten's anal area is washed by its mother, or in the case of an orphan, by a human or feline substitute, a kitten will never learn how to urinate and defecate and will die as a result. A clean, well-kept coat is a sign of good health, and one sign of illness is the shabby or unkempt appearance that results from loss of interest in grooming.

To remove dead hair and skin, cats lick themselves. Their tongues are covered with projections called papillae, which give a cat's tongue its rough sandpaper feel. To get to those hard-to-reach areas, your Manx will lick its paws, then run them over its ears, face, and whiskers to clean them. Your Manx will wash carefully between its toes and pull loose sheaths from its claws with its teeth.

Grooming is one of those tiny tasks that becomes big and unmanageable if not performed regularly and thoroughly. Cats are fastidious animals, well versed in the art of self grooming, and they are notorious for washing themselves, sometimes incessantly, by spending a good many of their relatively short waking hours engaged in the activity. A favorite grooming time among cats is after a meal or just before taking a nap. You may notice your Manx taking a quick lick right after it conducts itself with less grace than is ordinarily expected of cats.

Hair and There

As your Manx washes itself, it will ingest loose hair and swallow it. If you don't remove the loose or dead hair before your Manx has a chance to devour it for dessert, the hair will build up and form entwined wads called hairballs. Hairballs, if not regurgitated, lodge along your cat's digestive tract, causing blockage. If the hairball becomes large and impassible, surgery will be required to remove it. Regular brushing and combing will help prevent the formation of hairballs. Offering your Manx an over-the-counter hairball remedy once or twice a week will keep the digestive skids greased and swallowed hair moving along. In lieu of hairball remedy, you may give your Manx a dab of white petroleum jelly for the same purpose.

Your Manx will shed all year long to some degree but may shed more in the spring and summer months. Dead hair and skin will fall off and be deposited on your floors, furniture, and your cat's favorite sleeping spots. By regularly removing your Manx's loose and dead hair you will find more of it on a hairbrush and less of it on your furniture. The time you spend grooming may result in less time spent vacuuming.

Bathing

Most cats seem to have an aversion to water, although you may find the opposite is true for your Manx, as long as the water is soapless. The good news is, you don't have to bathe your Manx on a regular basis unless you plan to exhibit. As an exhibitor, you will be required to bathe your Manx before each show, in which case it is best to accustom your Manx kitten to the water rites when it is young.

Before bathing your Manx, comb and brush it to remove any knots or tangles. Clip its nails. As you groom and bathe, talk to your Manx, pet it and make the experience a positive one. When bathing your Manx, use lukewarm water and a mild shampoo or flea products intended for use on a cat. Have all your bathing equipment on hand before you start. Keep towels handy to dry your cat and possibly you if your wet Manx gives a good shake. Place a towel or rubber mat on the bottom of the sink in which you intend to bathe your Manx. If your Manx really appears to be nervous and reluctant at the impending wet-down, place a screen over the sink on which it can stand and cling while the water runs into the sink below. Another option is to restrain your Manx by placing it in a harness and using a very short lead that can be tied to a handle in the bathtub, while you have both hands free to bathe and pet the cat.

Lightly wet your Manx's hair, rub in the shampoo and massage it into your cat's hair. Wipe its face, being careful not to get shampoo into its eyes, ears, or mouth. Rinse off all the soap when you are finished. A white vinegar rinse of 1/4 cup of vinegar to 4 quarts (3.81 liters) of water makes a good rinse. Towel your cat dry by pressing, not rubbing, the water out of its hair. To prevent loss of body heat from water trapped in your Manx's undercoat instead of protective air, keep it in a warm room until it is dry. Or, if your Manx will tolerate a blow-dryer, dry its hair with the blow-dryer on a low setting. If you exhibit at shows and must bathe your cat often, you may want to investigate electric drying cages in which a wet cat sits until dry.

Brushing and Combing

Your shorthaired or longhaired Manx, like its ancestors on the Isle of Man, has a thick double coat of hair with an undercoat that may become denser in cold weather or cold climates. The outer guard hairs are coarser in texture than the undercoat, which has a finer, softer texture. This

Manx take to water more willingly than most cats.

combination renders their winter coats water repellent, and the heavy undercoat provides excellent insulation against the cold. The Manx double coat is a part of the Manx standard (see page 85) and if you ever want to show your Manx, the quality and condition of its coat will play an important part in the judging. The texture of your Manx's coat may affect whether it mats and, conversely, how easy it is to groom. As in most breeds, the texture of the Manx's hair may vary depending on its color. Breeders attest to white and red cats as well as tabbies having the thickest, coarsest coats while black cats usually have a finer coat. In most breeds the dilute colors—blues, creams, with any combination of agouti, smoke, or piebald—have a softer texture than the other colors.

The essential equipment you will need to properly groom your Manx are a metal comb with wide spacing between the teeth, a soft-bristled brush, and a medium-bristled brush. Unless you have a longhaired Manx, the hair most likely will not tangle, even with the cottony undercoat, but regular combing makes certain matting does not happen. To keep your Manx cat's coat in good condition and help when the cat is shedding, use a metal comb with its teeth about .125 to .25 inch (.3 to .6 cm) apart. If you have a Manx with an exceptionally thick coat or a longhaired Manx, a wider toothed metal comb will make the process easier.

Begin combing your Manx in the direction the hair grows on back, sides, belly,

Keep the dryer on low and test it frequently to make sure it doesn't get too hot.

and rear, making sure you remove any particles of feces from its anal area. Occasionally you may find bits of fecal matter clinging to the hairs around the anus, even if your Manx has short hair. This happens most often on Manx with coats of dilute colors—specifically, blue, blue cream, and cream. Many cats despise having the backs of their legs and their underbellies combed, because this entails exposing their sensitive areas. Accustom your Manx to being groomed from kittenhood and make the experience a positive one, to minimize any acts of rebellion when you take out the brush and comb. Once you are certain that any tangles have been removed, comb the hair sideways to remove loose hair, then in the direction in which it grows, to make the coat lie flat. Once you've combed your Manx, use the soft brush to disperse its skin oils throughout the coat to give it a natural shine. During shedding season, you might want to use a slicker brush to remove excess hair and enable your Manx to grow a nice show coat. Once your Manx's coat is in condition, use the medium brush to remove loose hair. Undercoat rakes, designed to strip a cat of the undercoat and

Show cats like this beautiful solid white Manx have coats that are the result of good care and nutrition. Before a show, a Manx must be bathed and brushed.

prevent matting, should not be used on a Manx because the lack of a double coat is a serious show fault. If you can't find the appropriate combs and brushes for your Manx locally, try a pet supply catalog or one of the many vendor stands at cat shows.

The Pedicure

Cats have inherited their need for sharp claws from their days in the wild when they had to hunt, kill prey, and defend themselves from attackers, whether they be other cats or wild animals. Your indoor warrior will keep its nails sharp by scratching them on surfaces within your home and by pulling off dead sheaths with its teeth. A scratching post will help your Manx sharpen its claws, but frequent pedicures will reduce potential damage to your furniture and carpets. If you intend to exhibit your Manx, you must clip its claws before the show. Most judges don't take too kindly to a cat that sinks its claws into their arms during inspection. If that occurs, you may find your potential award winner sitting it out in the benching area instead of accepting the rosette that you know in your heart it deserves.

The best clippers for trimming a cat's nails are designed for that purpose and available in pet stores, catalogs, or at cat shows. In addition to nail trimmers, the only other equipment you may need is an extra pair of hands. Nail trimming is easiest when one person holds the cat, and the other trims the cat's nails. To trim your Manx's nails, press the paw between your thumb and forefingers to extend the claws.

Dental care can be as simple as using a piece of gauze to clean your Manx's teeth.

Look closely at the claw, and you will see a pinkish area containing blood vessels, called the quick. Insert the claw into the clipper, being careful not to trim below the quick. Repeat the process for each claw. Have a styptic pencil handy to stop bleeding in case you nick a blood vessel.

The Declawing Debate

One of the most controversial issues among pet owners is whether to declaw a cat. Even veterinarians these days are getting into the fray. Declawing is the process of removing the last one or two tiny terminal bones of a cat's toe along with the claw to keep the cat from scratching furniture, curtains, and people. Proponents of declawing say it is preferable to offering the offending animal up for adoption or resale. They also point to the fact that veterinarians routinely perform the surgery and that most cats recover from it. Opponents feel that declawing is mutilation and that the declawed cat can suffer irreparable mental harm after the surgery. They also point to unsuccessful procedures that result in long-term bleeding when the cat walks and moves its toes. In some cases, the claws grow back.

Every cat owner must decide about declawing after discussing it with a veterinarian. If you intend to show your Manx, however, it must have its claws intact to conform to the

breed standard. If scratching is a problem, an alternative to declawing is to train your Manx to use a scratch post. For the Manx that resists its lessons, a solution could be a product available from veterinarians—tiny caps that an owner puts over each claw and replaces periodically when they fall off.

Brushing your Manx will remove dead hair and skin.

Regular grooming sessions enable you to keep up with your Manx's physical condition, find parasites, and detect any potential health problems early when they can be treated more easily. Although not intended to replace regular veterinary care, a home health exam should be a part of your grooming session along with basic combing and brushing. Place your cat on a table or bathroom vanity to make it easier for you to conduct the exam.

Visual Inspection

While grooming, inspect your Manx's coat for external parasites such as fleas or ticks. You will be able to detect fleas from any minuscule particles that fall off your cat as you rake your fingers through its coat. Composed of flea feces and dried blood, flea

dirt is a sure sign that fleas have been feasting on your Manx. If you detect fleas, consult your veterinarian.

As you run your fingers through your Manx's hair, check for abrasions or skin lesions that might indicate excessive self grooming or skin or coat problems caused by allergies. Look for any hair loss, especially on the inside of your Manx's thighs or at the base of the tail—two places where cats often wash more often than they should. Cats can be allergic to things in the environment, cleaning products, or even the food they eat, so finding the source of the allergy and eliminating from your Manx's diet or from the environment it is the best way to stop the excessive grooming or other allergic responses.

As your cat ages, feel the skin for any lumps or bumps

under the skin that may signal the onset of benign or cancerous tumors. Conducting a massage is the best way to feel for lumps, and your Manx will enjoy the experience. If you detect any abnormal conditions, discuss your findings with your veterinarian.

Eyes

The eyes are the doorway to the soul, the old saying goes. It's no different for your feline companion than it is for your human ones. When you give your Manx a home health exam, visually inspect your Manx's eyes. They should be clear and bright, and the third eyelid located in the inner corner or each eye should be barely visible. If your Manx injures an eye or has an illness such as conjunctivitis, the inner eyelid can become reddened, inflamed and raised, partially covering the eyeball. Tearing may indicate that your Manx has scratched its eye or has something in it. Minor tearing will clear up quickly. Discharge from your Manx's eyes is a sign of illness and should be checked by your veterinarian. Wiping off the discharge with warm water on a clean cloth is all that is needed to

A Manx relaxes in a drying cage after a grooming session.

remove it from your Manx's face. Like all cats, your Manx may occasionally have matter in the corner of its eyes. This is common, and the matter can be wiped off carefully with a clean cloth or your finger.

Ears

Examine your Manx's ears. The inside of the ears should be clean and pink. If you detect black or brown material that resembles dirt, it could be a sign that your Manx has ear mites. Although mites can be treated easily, early detection is the best way to rid your cat of these tiny, pesky creatures. Redness, sores or scabs in the ears, head shaking, or detectable odor emanating from the ears signals that something is wrong. If you detect any of these conditions, seek veterinary help.

Nose

If you see discharge coming from your Manx's nose, it could be a sign of respiratory illness. An occasional sneeze may simply mean that your Manx is reacting to dust particles or other environmental pollutants, but constant sneezing along with nasal discharge is cause for a veterinary visit. Respiratory illnesses are easily corrected, but if the condition is allowed to fester, the illness may be harder to treat.

Teeth

Look at your Manx's teeth. Like you, your Manx can suffer from the buildup of tartar and plaque. Left untreated, plaque can cause your Manx to develop gingivitis (inflammation of the gums) and periodontitis (inflammation

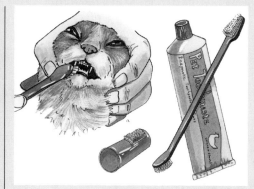

Examine your Manx's teeth whenever you brush them.

of the tooth socket lining), especially as it ages. Removing the buildup once it occurs must be done by a veterinarian while the cat is under anesthetic. Manufacturers recently have introduced food products and treats developed to help maintain dental health. Over-the-counter and veterinary prescribed products exist to help keep your Manx's teeth cleaned. Some are cat-sized toothbrushes with toothpaste developed for use on your cat. Rubber devices the size of large thimbles that have tiny projections on them can be put over your finger and rubbed lightly over your cat's teeth. A clean, wet terrycloth wash cloth or a piece of gauze will work as well. Before embarking on a feline dental plan, discuss the options with your veterinarian. And don't use human toothpaste on your cat. Human toothpaste was meant to be spit out rather than swallowed, so your cat may get an upset stomach if it ingests something it wasn't meant to eat.

The World of the Cat Fancy

Once you've purchased a Manx cat, whether it be show quality or pet quality, you most likely will become a cat fancier interested in participating in the world of the cat fancy. Cat fanciers are individuals who have a love for purebred cats, seek to perfect their breed of choice through controlled breeding programs, and promote the breed through competitions called cat shows. Participating in the cat fancy is something that can be done on many levels, appealing to the novice cat fancier as well as the experienced breeder.

Associations and Clubs

More than half a dozen cat associations in the United States and Canada and additional ones around the world maintain the pedigrees of the cats and kittens of its members and guarantee that future offspring can be registered and ancestors traced (see page 100). National associations as well as regional clubs are nonprofit organizations interested in promoting pedigreed cats and the welfare of cats in general. Many clubs designate a local animal welfare organization as recipient of proceeds from the show it is sponsoring. Members of the cat registries and clubs actively advance spay/neuter awareness in their communities, and many of their members become active volunteers at local animal shelters.

One of the benefits of your newfound status as a cat fancier is the sense of belonging and networking that occurs when you join a cat club affiliated with one of the national purebred cat associations. You will meet other owners of pedigreed cats as well as those who have chosen to breed them. As a Manx owner, you may be able to join a national association as an individual member or become affiliated with it via a local club, depending on the rules of the association in which you are interested. Each association approaches registering and competing in different ways, so investigate to find the right one for you. Some breeders and exhibitors register and compete in multiple associations, but competition points earned in one do not carry over to another.

Breed councils or committees of breeders knowledgeable and experienced in the breed serve as advisory bodies within the association to which they belong. Breed councils are responsible for the continued development of the breed. They recommend changes and obtain approval from the registry for modifications to the breed standard.

The American Manx Club

Manx breeders and owners can join the American Manx Club (AMC), a national organization affiliated with the Cat Fanciers' Association, Inc. The objectives of the AMC are to encourage the breeding and showing to the standard of Manx Cats; to sponsor shows and promote interest regarding breeding, exhibiting, care, and knowledge of the Manx Cat; to cultivate friendship and common interest among the members; to advance in every way possible the welfare of breeders and exhibitors, and to promote the welfare of all cats; and to give awards to high-scoring Manx in a given CFA show season.

Membership in the AMC is open to Manx lovers and breeders, but because the focus is on breeding and the association is with the Cat Fanciers' Association, members typically are Manx breeders associated with CFA. Information and a membership application are available on the AMC web page (see page 101). The AMC publishes a quarterly newsletter, *Manx Tales*.

Cat Shows

One of the most exciting activities associated with the cat fancy is attending and participating in cat shows. The primary purpose of cat shows is competition for awards and prizes, but they are also the only place where breeders obtain authoritative feedback on how well their cats meet breed standards. If you decide to breed cats, it is critical that you show them.

Cat shows are also places where breeders, cat owners, and cat product vendors congregate to show off their wares to an interested public or to each other, whether they be furry, four-footed prime breed specimens or products intended to make the lives of cats and owners fun and easy.

In 1871, the exhibition held in London's Crystal Palace marked the birth of the cat fancy. Although smaller regional cat shows had been held for several years, the first major United States event didn't occur until 24 years later when a cat show at New York City's Madison Square Garden marked the start of the cat fancy in the United States. Cat shows are broken down into all-breed shows or specialty shows that feature cats of a particular breed or coat length. Shows usually occur over the weekend and can last for one, two, or more days.

Cat shows are typically sponsored by local clubs affiliated with national registries. To enter a show, a cat must be registered with the sponsoring registry. Shows are held virtually all year all over the country and around the world. National and international shows in which cats compete for championships and national awards

Judge at a cat show gives spectators a good look at a Manx.

are sponsored by the national cat associations and are held near the end of the show season.

Attending a few shows as a spectator is advisable before jumping feet first into competition. As a spectator at a cat show, you will learn about cats, new cat-related products, and what constitutes a superb specimen of the breed. You also will learn about the local club and national association sponsoring the show. If you purchased a show-quality kitten or cat from a breeder, he or she will help you get started. A breeder's cattery reputation is on the line when you show your Manx, so make sure that the breeder has approved of the kitten you purchased being exhibited. If your Manx was sold as a pet, find out about showing it in the household pet category.

Entering a Show

Before entering a cat show, your Manx must be registered with the association sponsoring the show. Registry of kittens may vary from breeder to breeder and association to association. If you purchased an unregistered Manx kitten, it may be eligible to enter a show unregistered, but adult cats, to be eligible to compete, must be registered. In The International Cat Association, Inc. (TICA), however, an unregistered adult can enter a show one time on a trial basis before being required to be registered with the association.

Dates, locations, and entry fees of cat shows are advertised in the major cat publications as well as on the World Wide Web home pages of the cat registries. Obtain a copy of the show rules and contact the entry clerk to request a show flyer and entry form. After you send the completed form and fees, you will receive confirmation by mail.

Competition becomes steeper as a cat progresses from local or regional shows to national and international competitions. Every cat entering a show must be healthy, in prime physical condition, and an excellent example of the breed. Your Manx must be free of parasites and contagious diseases, have been vaccinated for rabies, and, in some cases, may be required to pass a veterinary inspection before the show.

Each show has several independently running judging rings, the number of which is determined by the sponsoring club or association. Each ring is presided over by a judge who is trained and licensed by the sponsoring association in either specific breeds and categories or all breeds and categories. Cats compete against the standard developed for the breed and they are judged with other cats of the same breed or type. As the show progresses, cats that have won against other cats of their breed or type compete for best of show categories with cats of other breeds and types. Depending on the rules of the association in which you are exhibiting, award categories may include:

Championship: unaltered, pedigreed cats eight months of age or older.

Premiership: spayed or neutered cats eight months of age or older.

Kitten: pedigreed kittens aged four to eight months.

Provisional or NBC (New Breed or Color): for breeds that have not yet achieved championship status.

AOV (Any Other Variety): registered cats that do not conform to breed standards.

These classes are divided and subdivided by color, breed, sex, age, and championship status. Prizes for winning in the various categories

Competing for ribbons and awards is one of the joys of entering cat shows. This red tabby male achieved a status of grand champion in the premier class.

include ribbons or rosettes. Once a cat has collected six first-place ribbons, it becomes a champion, after which it is eligible to compete against other champions to garner points for grand and supreme grand champion status. Depending on the show, cash prizes and trophies also may be given.

Upon arrival, your Manx will be assigned a number for that show, and when not in the show ring, will be housed in a cage in the benching area. Cages are typically decorated and carry the cattery name if the cats inside

are being shown by a breeder. Your Manx must be well-behaved and able to withstand the commotion, stress, and rigors of the show hall environment. When being judged, your Manx must be alert and playful, but maintain a passive attitude while being handled by the judge. In the benching area, your Manx must be able to cope with the close proximity of other cats as well as the adoring glances and comments of spectators attending the show.

When packing for a show, you will need a carrier for your cat, a litterbox, a cat bed or blanket, food and water dishes, a supply of food and water, grooming tools, a first aid kit, paper towels, terrycloth towels, vaccination certificates, and a show catalog. The show committee will provide cat litter. You might want to take decorations for your benching

The Manx Standard calls for a round head, with firm, round muzzle and prominent cheeks.

cage. A good cart with wheels will help you get from your car to the show hall without huffing and puffing.

The Manx Standard

Every accepted breed has a standard against which it is judged in competition. Although breed standards differ somewhat from registry to registry, they all attempt to define what the perfect breed specimen should look like. Standards provide a yardstick against which every breeder can measure his or her success at creating the perfectly defined cat. Every cat entered into competition should come close to meeting its breed standard. Below is the CFA standard for the Manx cat, and it is reprinted here with their kind permission.

Point Score

Head and Ears...25
Eyes 5
Body 25
Taillessness..5
Legs and Feet 15

Coat

Length 10
Texture..10
Color and Markings..5

General: the overall impression of the Manx cat is that of roundness; round head with firm, round muzzle and prominent cheeks; broad chest; substantial short front legs; short back which arches from shoulders to a round rump; great depth of flank and rounded, muscular thighs. The Manx should be alert, clear of eye, with a glistening, clean, well-groomed coat. They should be surprisingly heavy when lifted. Manx may be slow to mature and allowance should be made in young cats.

Head and ears: round head with prominent cheeks and a jowly appearance (more evident in adult males) that enhances the round appearance of the breed. In profile, head is medium in length with a gentle dip from forehead to nose. Well developed muzzle, very slightly longer than it is broad, with a strong chin. Definite whisker break with large, round whisker pads. Short, thick neck. Ears wide at the base, tapering gradually to a rounded tip. Medium in size in proportion to the head,

widely spaced and set slightly outward. When viewed from behind, the ear set resembles the rocker on a cradle. The furnishings of the ears are sparse in Shorthair Manx and full furnishings for Longhair Manx.

Eyes: large, round and full. Set at a slight angle toward the nose (outer corners slightly higher than inner corners). Ideal eye color conforms to requirements of coat color.

Body: solidly muscled, compact and well-balanced, medium in size with sturdy bone structure. The Manx is stout in appearance with broad chest and well-sprung ribs. The constant repetition of curves and circles give the Manx the appearance of great substance and durability, a cat that is powerful without the slightest hint of coarseness. Males may be slightly larger than females. Flank (fleshy area of the side between the ribs and hip) has greater depth than in other breeds, causing considerable depth to the body when viewed from the side. The short back forms a smooth, continuous arch from shoulders to rump, curving at the rump to form the desirable round look. Length of back is in proportion to the entire cat, height of hindquarters equal to length of body. Males may be somewhat longer. Because the Longhair Manx has longer coat over the rump area and breeches, the body may appear longer.

Taillessness: appearing to be absolute in the perfect specimen. A rise of bone at the end of the spine is allowed and should not be penalized unless it is such that it stops the judge's hand, thereby spoiling the tailless appearance of the cat. The rump is extremely broad and round.

Legs and feet: heavily boned, forelegs short and set well apart to emphasize the broad, deep chest. Hind legs much longer than forelegs, with heavy, muscular thighs and substantial lower legs. Longer hind legs cause the rump to be considerably higher than the shoulders. Hind legs are straight when viewed from behind. Paws are neat and round with five toes in front and four behind.

Coat length: Shorthair: double coat is short and dense with a well-padded quality due to the longer, open outer coat and the close cottony undercoat. Coat may be thinner during the summer months.

Coat texture: Shorthair: texture of outer guard hairs is somewhat hard, appearance is glossy. A softer coat may occur in whites and dilutes due to color/texture gene link but should not be confused with the silky texture found in the Longhair Manx.

Coat length: Longhair: the double coat is of medium length, dense and well padded over the main body, gradually lengthening from the shoulders to the rump. Breeches, abdomen and neck-ruff is usually longer than the coat on the main body. Cheek coat is thick and full. The collar-like neck-ruff extends from the shoulders, being bib-like around the chest. Breeches should be full and thick to the hocks in the mature cat. Lower leg and head coat (except for cheeks) should be shorter than on the main body and neck-ruff, but dense and full in appearance. Toe tufts and ear tufts are desirable. All things being equal in type, preference should be given to the cat showing full coating.

Coat texture: Longhair: coat is soft and silky, falling smoothly on the body yet being full and plush due to the double coat. Coat should have a healthy glossy appearance. Allowance to be made for seasonal and age variations.

Transfer to AOV: definite, visible tail joint. Long, silky coat on the Shorthair Manx or short, hard coat on the Longhair Manx.

Penalize: on the Longhair Manx, coat that lacks density, has a cottony texture or is of one overall length.

Disqualify: evidence of poor physical condition; incorrect number of toes; evidence of hybridization; evidence of weakness in the hindquarters.

Cats of All Colors

The Manx cat comes in colors too numerous to mention here. You will be able to find the Manx of your choice in solid colors, bicolors, tortoiseshell, calico, classic, mackerel tabby, shaded, and smoke combinations. Colorpoint colors, which indicate outcrossing with other breeds such as the Himalayan or Persian, are not allowed in CFA but can be shown in TICA and The American Cat Association (ACA).

When competing, remember that no two judges think alike, and the same judge may have a different opinion about your cat when he or she sees it at another show. Judging time is very brief, about 90 seconds, during which time the judge will attempt to evaluate your cat against the breed standard. No matter what the outcome, whether your cat wins a ribbon or not, learn from the experience. Competition should be healthy and fun. If you decide to exhibit your Manx, make the experience an enjoyable one.

BREEDING YOUR MANX

Why Would You Want To?

Ask reputable breeders, and they will tell you that there is one and only one reason for breeding cats: a love of the breed. The goal of a responsible breeder is to preserve and protect the chosen breed, and the goal of his or her breeding program is to improve the breed's conformation and type. A responsible breeder will compete in cat shows to provide a means of measuring that improvement. For the cats' health and well-being, responsible breeders keep the number of breeding animals within their catteries to a minimum and, in view of the millions of cats euthanized every year for lack of homes, prevent accidental pregnancies. They assume the full responsibility for the kittens they bring into the world, including providing veterinary and other care for them when they are young and finding good homes for them when they have reached 14 to 16 weeks of age. If good homes cannot be found, responsible breeders provide lifetime care for the animals that cannot be placed.

Food for Thought

There are some very compelling issues to consider before deciding to breed your Manx. Unaltered cats are unrelenting when it comes to getting sex. Estrus, or the heat cycle, is dependent on many factors including the amount of daylight. Females typically come into heat from March through September in the northern hemisphere, although it can occur at any time.

A female in heat exhibits annoying behaviors that include yowling, spraying, and body language that is designed to make her receptive to the male. When around a female in heat, a male will begin to spray its territory, and the resulting odor can be quite offensive to humans. Such behaviors may be difficult to live with.

It takes dedication, time, and energy to keep up with feline reproductive science as well as general veterinary medicine, genetics, behavior in a household that has several cats, and anything else that might improve the lives of cats. Responsible breeders are quite indefatigable in their resolve to keep abreast of current information pertaining to cat care, including reading veterinary journals and attending conferences and seminars.

Aside from the time and effort it takes simply to show your cats, carefully choose mates for your breeding felines, care for their offspring, and find good homes for them when the time comes, breeding requires a commitment on the part of the breeder to keep up with current information related to cats and their care.

Also, breeding is not inexpensive. You can buy a Manx more cheaply than you can breed one. Expenses include food, veterinary care, stud service if applicable, and cattery setup and maintenance. Pregnant queens may need veterinary assistance with birthing, cesarean sections, uterine inertia, and other unforeseen developments. Funds must be available to pay for health care during pregnancy and throughout the animals' lives. Add to that the association and registration fees as well as show and travel costs—a necessary part of breeding—and it becomes obvious that breeding requires a substantial financial commitment.

Breeding can be very rewarding when you see your first show cat become a grand champion, or even a regional or national winner, but it is a demanding job to help with delivery, wean the kittens, and keep them healthy during the months before they are old enough to go to a new home. There can be heartbreaks, too, if a female has trouble delivering or kittens are born with health problems. Working with living creatures means being aware of the worst that can happen. Death is part of life, but the responsible breeder attempts to minimize loss of life caused by genetic defects or poor conditions. A novice also needs to prepare for the expected emergency expenses, such as cesarean sections, diseases, and medical conditions requiring veterinary care.

A breeder should take care about expansion—too many cats will cause all of them to be unhappy; too few cats can result in illness among the ones who are to be bred. Females may develop infection of the uterus; males need to be sexually active or their health will suffer. And sometimes, no matter how many precautions you take or how diligent you are, you just are going to lose one. Under most circumstances, what you gain far outweighs what you stand to lose, but as a prospective breeder, you must consider that the unexpected may happen, too.

Occasionally, an owner of a female cat will say that he or she simply wants to allow the cat to have a litter of kittens before having it spayed. Having just one litter means nothing to the cat. Becoming pregnant and giving birth does not hold the same potential for emotional fulfillment as it might in a human female. Although cats are wonderful mothers to their kittens, sex and reproduction are biological functions rather than emotionally fulfilling ones. Your female Manx will not sit around and pine because she has no mate and, therefore, no kittens. Unless a female is a show cat and part of a breeding program, you may be contractually obligated to have her spayed to complete the registration process.

Another reason that cat owners often give is that they want their children to experience the miracle of birth. Most births are in the middle of the night when the children are usually in bed. Births that do not go smoothly can leave a bad impression on the young mind. If a child wants to see birthing of animals, there are instructional videos available at libraries. Animal shelters are inundated with pregnant females during the birthing season, and the shelters cry out for volunteers.

Spaying and Neutering

If your Manx is to be a pet, have it spayed or neutered to avoid contributing to the cat overpopulation problem. Estimates for the number of animals euthanized every year are as high as eight million. These animals find their way into shelters, and most are put to death because there are not enough homes for them. This figure does not include the countless numbers of cats that die homeless on the streets or the ones euthanized by veterinarians at the instructions of their owners because of health or behavior problems.

Responsible breeders avoid accidental breedings and do not produce kittens that are not intended to improve the quality of the Manx breed. Deciding to breed your Manx cat should be a decision that is made with careful consideration for your cat, its offspring, and the countless number of cats unable to find homes—an outcome you may face if you breed indiscriminately or continually produce only pet kittens.

Before You Start...

If you've weighed all the issues carefully, and you are sincere in your desire to pursue breeding Manx cats, there are a few preparations you should make. Following some simple guidelines recommended by top Manx breeders will help ensure your success in your breeding efforts.

Become involved: Most Manx breeders recommend that you begin your career in the cat fancy by purchasing an altered cat and showing it in the premiership class. This demonstrates your willingness to learn about the Manx breed before jumping into attempting to breed it. The premiership class is made up of some of the finest examples of Manx in existence. Many of them are on their second show careers, having become grand champions and then having produced kittens. Once their breeding career is over, they then can go out and reenter the show world, most often at their physical peak. By showing a premier, you learn exhibiting, grooming, handling, and what makes a champion Manx.

As part of the process, memorize the breed standard for the association in which you are showing. By showing in the premiership category, you can develop an understanding of why certain specimens are superior examples of the breed. The only reason to breed is to improve the breed; physical appearance, health, and temperament of kittens should be equal to or better than their parents'. In order to do that, one should have a good idea of what those desirable attributes should be and select cats to breed for those attributes. Any novice cat fancier must learn what the perfect cat of their breed looks like, how to evaluate a cat's faults, how to go about improving on the next generation. What is the head type you think is best? The body type? The coat? The temperament? The overall health? After you can make a good evaluation of a cat, you can confidently choose new breeding stock that is of superior quality and will work well with the bloodlines of your other cats.

It is recommended that you actively participate in at least one show season, which runs from May 1 to the end of April the following year in most associations. As with any large organization made up of people with differing views and opinions, showing often involves a certain amount of politics, which you as a prospective breeder can evaluate in terms of your willingness to become involved.

Work with a mentor: Working with an established breeder who has learned the art and craft of breeding will help you avoid many of the pitfalls that may cause newcomers to remain in the category of casual or backyard breeder or become so discouraged that they will quit breeding altogether. Manx breeders are only too willing to help a novice who has done his or her homework and has become knowledgeable about the breed, exhibiting, and the cat fancy. Becoming an apprentice to a breeder is the best way to begin for anyone wanting to breed cats, generally, and Manx, specifically. Talk to each breeder and ask for his or her best and worst experiences with the

This kitten's breeder found a home for it and all its littermates in advance of the breeding.

breed. Discuss the pedigree lines the breeder works with. An established breeder will help a newcomer learn about facilities, feeding, grooming, cost of caring for the cats, and sorting out the reasons to breed in the first place. A responsible breeder with whom you establish a relationship will be an ongoing source of information as well as someone to talk to about any problems that may arise.

Become informed: Before rushing into breeding your Manx, arm yourself with as much information as possible about cat breeding and genetics. There are several good books that should be in your personal library (see page 100).

Taking courses or attending seminars on breeding is another useful way to learn about cat breeding. *The Cat Fanciers' Journal* with the assistance of the American Association of Feline Practitioners (AAFP) has developed the

Cat Breeder Certification Program, a correspondence course that is available to anyone interested in becoming a reputable, responsible breeder. The course covers feline anatomy, physiology, bacteria, viruses, drugs, diseases, genetics, reproduction, showing, grooming, cattery management, contracts, and other topics important to breeders. Individuals taking the course receive several books on cat breeding and general cat care. The course includes a practical examination with a veterinarian and a final exam that is proctored by a librarian or teacher. Successful completion of the course results in certification. The cost of the course is $695, which includes a basic set of breeding reference books (see page 101).

In addition to the certification course, those interested in breeding can attend seminars. Universities that have veterinary schools often offer seminars on breeding, genetics, care, and behavior. Every year, the Cornell Feline Health Center at Cornell University in New York offers a seminar in feline behavior and breeding. The University of Pennsylvania veterinary school offers seminars in cat care and genetics in the spring and summer.

Plan your cattery: The facilities in which you house the cats will be an important part of your breeding program. Stud males and females in heat should be kept separate from other cats in your home. Once the queen has delivered, she and the kittens should be kept separate also until the kittens are weaned, although they will need plenty of contact and socialization with you. Once weaned, the kittens can become members of the household with all its rights and privileges until they are placed in new homes. Designing and building a cattery can be as simple or complex as you want it to be. Regardless of the cattery layout and size, other factors must be taken into consideration, such as ventilation, climate control, sanitation, lighting, and, if outdoors, shelter from the weather. If the pedigreed cat association to which you belong has a Cattery of Excellence program, obtain the standards that must be followed for the operation of the cattery and the care of the animals housed there. The CFA publishes as part of its Approved Cattery Environment Program a set of standards that covers the physical plant—food handling and transport, heating, ventilation, and air-conditioning—the primary enclosure and its construction, feeding and water, cleaning and sanitation, and the health care of the animals. Discuss with other breeders how they have set up their catteries. Ask yourself some questions about what you want to accomplish. Do you want the cattery to be a part of your home or a separate building? If it is a part of your home, will you want the cats to have outside runs in which they can play and relax? Are you likely to have more than one female pregnant at a time, and do you want to build separate birthing areas within the cattery for each of them? In the book *Feline Husbandry* author Niels C. Pedersen devotes an entire chapter to cattery design, layout, and ongoing management (see page 101). A cattery that begins with a simple design and can be expanded to house more breeding cats is a good way to start.

Know your local laws: Individual communities have breeding, multicat ownership and licensing laws that have to be considered before beginning a breeding program. In addition, municipalities have building codes, which govern the construction of new facilities on or additions to existing properties within the boundaries of the municipality. Before beginning a breeding program or building a cattery on your property, investigate the local laws that may govern the number of cats you have in your home and the operation of your cattery or require you to obtain a breeding license or a building permit.

The Perfect Mates

If you decide that you would like to breed Manx, obtain a female and send her to someone who provides stud service for mating. Because of potential health problems that may arise in intact males and females not engaged in reproduction, it is advisable that you not house a stud cat until you have several females in your cattery that you want to breed. In addition, most breeding males need to be caged or confined to a specific area where spraying will not be a problem. Occasionally, a male will not spray, but no one should count on this being the case.

The characteristics of cats, like all living organisms, are controlled by the complex interaction of their genetic makeup. The manner in which an organism's physical and behavioral traits are transmitted from parents to offspring is studied in the science of genetics—a branch of biology which began in 1900 when researchers rediscovered the work of Gregor Mendel, an Austrian monk who, 40 years earlier, described the pattern of inheritance in garden peas. Mendel believed that each parent has pairs of units in its chromosomes but contributes only one unit from each pair to its offspring. These genes, which are inherited from each parent, provide a set of instructions for building a new, uniquely individual cat.

Genetics: A knowledge of genetics and how pairings reproduce certain characteristics in their offspring is fundamental to cat breeding and enables the breeder to scientifically determine beforehand what kittens of specific mothers and fathers should look like. The genes inherited from an animal's parents are called its genotype. The physical appearance and characteristics are its phenotype. Because certain characteristics are governed by dominant genes and others by recessive ones, predicting the outcome of pairings depends on knowing not only what the parents looked like, but also what the grandparents, great-grandparents, and so on through several generations looked like and the kinds of offspring they produced.

A cat's genetic makeup determines all its features, from the shape of its body to the roundness of its eyes and the color of its hair. Many of the books recommended in the Information section (pages 100–101) will give the prospective breeder a head start, as will the breeder's certification course, in learning the complex science of genetics and how pairing individual genes results in certain outcomes in offspring.

Determine your female's strong points and weak points. For example, if you have a female with a good head but a less than round, full, sturdy body, you will want to look for a male who is deep in the flank and with good bone and weight. If you don't have roundness of eye, head, and body, look for a male with those characteristics. If you have what you consider an excellent female according to type, you select a male who is her match, and who has a sweet, gentle temperament. If her coat needs work, go for a male with good double coat, and so on.

Before choosing a breeding female or a stud, learn about the bloodlines to avoid some of the problems that may appear in some of them. Although most of the United States or European Manx lines currently are not experiencing any genetic-related health problems, certain types of breeding practices may result in reappearance of problems, and certain pedigree lines may be prone to them.

When trying to determine an appropriate mate for your Manx female, consider a multitude of factors. Ask to see a five- to six-generation pedigree to determine what is behind the cats, a current picture of the male and, if possible, pictures of him as a young kitten. Look for the number of grand champions produced, number of line breedings (breeding cats related back three-four or more generations), number of outcrosses and any close matings (brother and sister, father and daughter, for example) that may have been done. Expect to have seen the male at cat shows. Determine what kinds of kittens he produced with other females and what lines he works best with. Go to the breeder's home and see how the cats are kept. If possible, see what cats were behind him on his family tree.

Taillessness: You also need to know the health history of the cats behind your cat as well as the one you are considering as stud. Tail-lessness has long been thought to be the result of the genetic defect that can cause associated weaknesses affecting the whole spinal column. This preconception has been challenged during the last few years by American and European breeders who have greatly decreased occurrences of weaknesses through the selective use of sound cats. Does the line produce healthy kittens or are there illnesses which appear? What is the percentage of defective kittens, and what is the defect—spinal bifida, megacolon, or weak hind legs, for example? Consider your female's temperament—is she sweet or a bit on the feisty side? Shy or lazy? Select a male who will improve upon those characteristics. If you observe that your female is excessively temperamental, shy or touchy, consider not breeding her at all, since temperament does pass along from parents to their offspring. With any litter, you could get defective kittens or kittens with disagreeable temperaments. In the worst case scenario, the defective or deformed kittens must be humanely euthanized. At best, kittens with health problems or testy temperaments are not placeable and will rely on you for their continued care.

Line breeding and inbreeding: Line breeding involves mating cats with the same family tree or pedigree. Inbreeding involves mating cats that are directly related such as mother and son, father and daughter. Although a type or "look" cannot be made with random breedings, a breeder must be judicious in the use of relatives with the like characteristics desired. As with most of life, too much of a good thing can result in problems. In breeding, too much of a characteristic can reinforce not only the good features but also bad ones. Carefully consider close-relative breeding. Close family breeding can fix a characteristic or look (round heads, big bodies, or good coats, for example), but, if a breeder chooses to do this, he or she should be certain that neither line has produced deformities or abnormalities. Inbreeding within a feline family unit will reproduce the problem multifold, if a problem exists. Line breeding within a pedigree will do the same. Because the Manx gene is an imperfect penetrant, it acts uniquely on each individual, but if a cat's littermates or parents' littermates have had deformities, then the potential for the deformity showing up in the kittens is great. In most cases, breeders do not do immediate family breeding (father/daughter, mother/son, full-sibling littermates). Half-sibling matings may be successful as long as the cats are related only on one side of the pedigree, and the other side is completely unrelated. The cats making up the pedigree should be as clear of deformities, abnormalities and health problems as possible. In other words, none of the littermates had problems, and none of the parents' littermates had problems.

The Manx gene can produce kittens with varying tail lengths in one litter while only the rumpy and rumpy-riser can be shown in most

associations. Predicting the number of rumpies in a litter of kittens produced by certain parental pairings is an inexact science, at best, but examining the line of cats before selecting a mate for your Manx will help ensure that the number of tailed cats is kept to a minimum. Some Manx breeders suggest that a new breeder get a stumpy or riser female and a rumpy male of a completely different line. Assuming that both lines are free of health problems, it is safe to breed rumpy to rumpy. If a particular male seems to produce more rumpies than tails with any queen to whom he's mated, then chances are he comes from a line that has done the same. If the line produces more than average rumpies, or rumpy-risers, then keeping to the line with occasional outcrossings will produce the desired absence of a tail.

Contracts: Once you have chosen a male with which your female will breed, expect to

A playful Manx calico kitten explores the world around it.

sign a contract with the owner of the male setting forth conditions of the breeding, including the cost, reciprocal breeding, leasing the female for a litter, guaranteeing number of living kittens in the litter, and other considerations. It is customary for two live kittens to be guaranteed, and if not, a rebreeding or refund should be specified, and whether a rebreeding is to the same male or a different male. By live kittens, it is meant that they will make it to at least a specified number of months in age. A kitten that lives for three days before dying, for example, is not considered a live kitten. A kitten that must be put down for cause isn't considered live, either, although it might live for four to five weeks.

Timing Is Everything

Choosing the right time to mate your female depends on when she goes into heat. The estrus cycle can depend on many factors, including the amount of daylight, which, when it reaches 12 hours, will trigger the hormonal system signifying the beginning of the reproductive cycle.

Your Manx may go into heat several times during the breeding season. The estrus cycle has four stages, the length of which may vary from queen to queen. The first stage is called proestrus, during which time the queen's appetite may increase, and she becomes more affectionate and utters short, chirpy calls. Proestrus lasts from one to two days. In estrus, the second stage of the heat cycle, the queen becomes receptive to a male, and it is during this time that she should be mated. Signs of estrus are unmistakable. Your female will make more and louder noise which will attract toms. She will become increasingly affectionate with you, rub around your legs and roll on the floor. You will observe her walking with her rear slightly elevated. Estrus lasts from four to six days. During estrus, a female should be mated. Unlike humans, cats don't ovulate until they copulate, so the pair may have to mate several times before the female becomes pregnant. Allow her to be with the stud for about a week. During the third stage, interestrus, a queen will aggressively reject any more suitors. If mating was unsuccessful, the queen will remain in interestrus for one to two weeks after which she will begin the cycle all over again with proestrus. If she became pregnant, kittens will be born in about 63 days. The last cycle is anestrus, a time during which the reproductive cycle is simply at rest, usually from October through February.

Pregnancy

If a woman suspects she is pregnant, determining it conclusively can be as simple as going to the local drug store for a home pregnancy test. No such test exists to determine whether two cats have successfully mated. During the first few weeks of pregnancy, you may notice your female gaining weight. By the fifth week, her nipples may become pink and more clearly noticeable. By the following week, you will be able to feel the kittens heads inside the female's uterus. Palpation should be done gently and carefully by a veterinarian. Ultrasound will detect kittens as early as two weeks or so during gestation and heartbeats are detectable within three weeks.

During pregnancy, a queen safely can engage in moderate activity and exercise, although she should be restricted from climbing to high places. Feed the pregnant queen food developed for kittens, which contains extra protein, during the first four weeks of pregnancy. During the last week or two before delivery, feed the queen several smaller meals during the day if she has difficulty consuming her normal portions of food.

Delivery

In your cattery you will have a kittening box in which a pregnant queen can give birth. The box should be clean, dry, and warm. Keep the area at a temperature of 85°F (53°C) during delivery and for a week thereafter. Lower the temperature five degrees each week until it is at 70°F (38°C). The queen should be housed in the kittening area before delivery to keep her from choosing a nesting area somewhere else in the house such as in a closet or in your bed.

Blessed Event

The first stage of delivery may last 12 or more hours. During this time, a queen's cervix dilates and opens the birth canal. On the day of delivery the queen will begin licking her anal area, and her appetite may decrease. At complete dilation, the kitten slides into the queen's vagina. Within about 30 minutes, the kitten is born. Subsequent kittens are born about 15 minutes apart on the average, but it can be as close as 5 minutes and as far apart as 3 hours. More than 3 hours may signify a problem, so keep track of her delivery. Each kitten is born in an amniotic sac, which the queen will tear open and consume. She will lick and clean each newborn, which removes fluid from their mouths and noses and helps stimulate breathing.

A Manx litter may range from three to five kittens. As mentioned in an earlier chapter, kittens that inherit the Manx gene from both parents die in the womb, reducing the litter size. If a queen comes from a large litter, and her mother also came from a large litter, then she probably will produce a larger than average litter. According to the genetic grid, rumpies or risers bred to rumpies will produce an average of three kittens compared with the average litter of four or more for other tail lengths.

Most deliveries go smoothly without human intervention. Occasionally problems develop such as a larger than normal kitten becoming stuck in the birth canal, or uterine inertia—the uterus becoming too tired to contract. Signs of problems can include 60 minutes of intense labor with no associated births, a kitten visible in the birth canal for ten or more minutes, fresh bleeding for ten minutes during or after delivery and more than three hours between kittens. In such circumstances, it is best to call your veterinarian. In some cases, he or she will recommend performing a cesarean section to complete the delivery process.

Care of the Kittens

Newborn kittens are born without the ability to see or hear, and they depend on their mother's licking of their anal areas to learn how to urinate and defecate. They spend a great deal of time sleeping and nursing and rely on their mother's milk not only to provide nourishment but also to help their undeveloped immune systems fight disease and infection.

Newborns weigh about 3.5 ounces (99 g) at birth. They grow at a rate indicated by the chart below. To help determine if your kittens are growing, weigh each of them daily for the first two weeks of life and keep track of their ages and weights on a chart. A useful weighing device is an inexpensive kitchen or pastry scale that records weight in ounces or grams, with a bowl on top in which you can place each kitten to weigh it. After two weeks of age, weigh them every three days for an additional two weeks. If a kitten fails to gain weight, a contributing factor may be the mother not producing enough milk, in which case you will have to intercede with hand feedings. During lactation, a mother cat needs two to three times more calories than before she became pregnant. If she does not get the proper amount of calories and proper nutrition, she will not be able to produce enough milk.

At about eight weeks, kittens weigh about two pounds (.9 k), and they should be given their first series of kitten shots. Most health problems, if they are to occur, will show up within the first few weeks of life. Once a kitten reaches the age of three months, most genetic-related problems will become apparent. At three to four months, their conformation to the breed standard will be more easily ascertained. At that time, kittens can be placed in new homes.

Growing Up

Socialization is an important part of raising kittens. Be certain to handle the kittens for at least 20 minutes a day, take them out beginning at the age of four weeks or so for little excursions. Invite people in and bring the kittens into the living room to be handled. To acclimate the kittens to children, allow your children to gently handle them. Cats in homes with children get used to more noise and bustle than cats living with an adult or two homes. Rent or borrow a neighbor's kid if you don't have any of your own.

Parting Is Such Sweet Sorrow

Kittenhood is a period of joy and wonder. Seeing your Manx kittens being born and watching them grow is a delight to behold. When the kittens are three to four months old, you will want to begin thinking about placing them in new, loving homes. Although it may be difficult to part with your tiny charges, placing a healthy, well-adjusted Manx kitten in the home of another person who loves the breed just as much as you do provides another level of satisfaction and enjoyment.

Shortly after birth, determine the colors and sexes of your kittens. To determine sex, lift up the kitten's tail. Just below the base of the tail is the first opening, or anus. If the kitten is female, a vertical slit, the vulva, is immediately below the anus. In a male kitten, the tip of the penis is in a small opening about .5 inch (1.3 cm) below the anus. Between the two openings are the scrotal sacs or testicles, which may not be felt until the kitten is about six weeks old.

Register the litter at birth with the association to which your female is registered. The pedigreed cat association will return to you a packet of blue slips, one matching the sex and color for each of the kittens in the litter. The blue form along with a three-to-five generation pedigree will accompany each kitten sold to a new owner.

As each kitten ages to three or four months, you will be able to determine how closely it conforms to the Manx standard and whether you want to show or breed the cat. For another opinion, consult with the breeder who has become your mentor. Show or breeding cats can become part of your breeding program or sold as show animals at a higher cost than pet Manx. Those that are pet Manx should be altered before sale or sold with a contract that stipulates that they be altered by the new owner's veterinarian. Many Manx breeders alter every one of their cats that do not become part of their cattery, stipulating that those that conform to standard can be shown in the premiership class.

Before offering your kittens for sale, have them examined again by a veterinarian to certify their good health. Make certain that they have had their complete series of kitten shots and have the health checkup information available to present to the buyer. Screen potential buyers carefully when they call with inquiries (see pages 22–23). You have invested a lot of time and effort to produce sound, healthy Manx kittens and you want them to go to good homes with people who will care for them properly for their entire life.

INFORMATION

Useful Addresses

American Association of Cat Enthusiasts, Inc. (AACE)
Box 213
Pine Brook, IL 07058
913-335-6717
info@aaceinc.org
http://www.aaceinc.org

American Cat Association (ACA)
81901 Katherine Avenue
Panaorama City, CA 91402
818-781-5656

American Cat Fanciers Association (ACFA)
P.O. Box 203
Point Lookout, MO 65726
417-334-5430
info@acfacat.com
http://www.acfacat.com

Australian Cat Federation, Inc. (ACF)
Post Office Box 3305
Port Adelaide SA 5015
Phone: 08 8449 5880
http://www.fam.aust.com/aus-catfed/index.html

Canadian Cat Association (CCA)
220 Advance Blvd., Suite 101
Brampton, Ontario,
Canada L6T 4J5

Cat Fanciers' Association (CFA)
Box 1005
Manasquan, NJ 08736
cfa@cfainc.org
http://www.cfainc.org

Cat Fanciers' Federation (CFF)
Box 661
Gratis, OH 45330
513-787-9009
http://www.cffinc.org

Federation Internationale Feline (FIFE)
c/o Ms. Penelope Bydlinski
Little Dene
Lenham Heath
Maidstone, Kent
GB-ME17 2BS
Phone 44 1622 850913
E-mail 106353.540@com-puserve.com
http://www2.dk-online.dk/users/kriste_m/fife/fifemain.htm

The International Cat Association, Inc. (TICA)
Box 2684
Harlingen, TX 78551
210-428-8046
http://www.tica.org/

Miscellaneous Organizations

National Animal Poison Control Center
College of Veterinary Medicine
University of Illinois
Urbana, IL 61801

Adverse Drug Experiences Reporting System
Center for Veterinary Medicine
U.S. Food and Drug Administration
7500 Standish Place
Rockville, MD 20855-2773

Books

Behavior
Ackerman, Lowell, DVM, et al. *Cat Behavior and Training: Veterinary Advice for Owners.* Neptune, New Jersey: TFH Publications, 1996.

Shojai, Amy. *Competibility: A Practical Guide to Building a Peaceable Kingdom Between Cats and Dogs.* New York: Three Rivers Press, 1998.

Wright, John C., PhD, and Judi Wright Lashnits. *Is Your Cat Crazy? Solutions from the Casebook of a Cat Therapist.* New York: Macmillan Publishing Company, 1994.

Breeding and Genetics
Gilberson, Elaine Wenner. *A Feline Affair: Guide to Raising and Breeding Purebred Cats.* Loveland, Colorado: Alpine Publications, 1993.

Keeping kittens until they are three to four months old enables breeders to evaluate their health and conformation to breed standard.

Gould, Laura L. *Cats Are Not Peas: A Calico History of Genetics*. New York: Copernicus Books, 1996.

Moore, Ann. *Breeding Purebred Cats*. Madison, Wisconsin: Abraxas Publishers, 1987.

Pedersen, Niels C., editor. *Feline Husbandry: Diseases and Management in the Multi-Cat Environment*. Goleta, California: American Veterinary Publications, 1991.

Rice, Dan, DVM. *The Complete Book of Cat Breeding*. Hauppauge, New York: Barron's, 1997.

Robinson, Roy, F.I. Biol. *Genetics for Cat Breeders*. New York: Pergamon Press, 1991.

Vella, Carolyn and John McGonagle, Jr. *Breeding Pedigreed Cats*. New York: Howell Book House, 1997.

Wright, Michael and Sally Walters. *The Book of the Cat*. New York: Summit Books, 1980.

Exhibiting

Vella, Carolyn and John McGonagle, Jr. *In the Spotlight*. New York: Macmillan General Reference, 1990.

Health Care

Anderson, Robert, DVM, and Barbara Wrede. *Caring for Older Cats and Dogs: Extending Your Pet's Healthy Life*. Charlotte, Vermont: Williamson Press, 1990.

McGinnis, Terri, DVM. *The Well Cat Book: The Classic Comprehensive Handbook of Cat Care*. New York: Random House, 1993.

Mammato, Bobbie, DVM, MPH. *Pet First Aid*. The American Red Cross and The Humane Society of the United States, 1997.

Thornton, Kim Campbell and John Hamil, DVM. *Your Aging Cat*. New York: Howell Book House, 1997.

Manx Cats

Swantek, Marjan. *The Manx Cat*. Neptune, New Jersey: TFH Publications, 1987.

Cat Breeders' Correspondence Course

For information, contact *The Cat Fanciers' Journal*, P.O. Box 3077, Sumas, WA 98295, Tel: 604-796-0187; Fax: 604-796-3144

Magazines

CATS
2 News Plaza
P.O. Box 1790
Peoria, IL 61656
309-682-6626

Cat Fancy
P.O. Box 6050
Mission Viejo, CA 92690
714-855-8822

Cat World
10 Western Road
Soreham-By-Sea
West Sussex BN43 5WD England

Internet and Web Resources

American Manx Club with links to members' pages: http://www.manxcats.com/amc.htm

Cat Fanciers' Association: http://www.cfainc.org

The Fanciers Breeder Referral List: http://www.fanciers.com

Pet Planet Cats: http://petplanet.nl

Most pedigreed cat associations maintain a presence on the Web.

I N D E X

The Author

Karen Commings, a columnist and contributing editor for *Cat Fancy* magazine, has been writing professionally for more than ten years. She is a member of the Cat Writers' Association and winner of four Muse Medallions for her works, which have appeared in every major cat magazine. She is the author of two books, *Shelter Cats* and *The Shorthaired Cat: An Owner's Guide to a Happy, Healthy Pet.*

Cover Photos

Landmark Stock Exchange: front cover; inside front cover; Nance Photography: inside back cover; Scott McKiernan: back cover.

Photo Credits

Norvia Behling: pages 4, 12, 92, 88, 96; Tara Darling: pages 9, 16, 28 bottom, 36 top, bottom, 37 bottom, 100; Isabelle Francais: pages 2–3, 17, 29 top, 76, 80; Sherman and Sandra Ross: page 20 top, 37 top, 84; McKiernan/ZUMA: pages 20 bottom, 24, 45 bottom, 56, 72, 85; Bonnie Nance: pages 32, 77 top, bottom; Donna Coss: pages 40, 52, 60; Kris Dickenson: page 57. All other photos provided by the author.

Important Note

This pet owner's guide tells the reader how to buy and care for a Manx. The author and the publisher consider it important to point out that the advice given in the book is meant primarily for normally developed kittens from a reputable breeder; that is, cats of excellent physical health and good temperament.

Anyone who adopts a fully grown Manx should be aware that the animal has already formed its basic impressions of human beings. The new owner should watch the cat carefully, including its behavior toward humans, and should meet the previous owner. If the cat comes from a shelter, it may be possible to get some information on its background and peculiarities.

When you handle cats, you may get scratched or bitten. If this happens, have a doctor treat the injuries immediately.

Make sure your cat receives all the necessary immunizations and wormings. Otherwise, its health may be endangered, and it could even pass on some diseases to humans.

Acknowledgments

The author wishes to express her sincere appreciation and thanks to Sherman W. Ross, president of the American Manx Club and owner of Tahame Manx cattery, and Dayle Hall, owner of Tra-March cattery, without whose assistance this book could not have been written. Thanks also go to Gale Thomas-Goodman (Vagary cattery), Becky Cotter (Cottori-Manx), Susan Murphy (Katskans), Jean Brown (Romannx), Richard Cullen (Blarney Manx), Mimy Sluiter (Moirawin Manx, the Netherlands), Ms. Sue Critchley of the Mann Cat Sanctuary on the Isle of Man, John W. Daugherty, DVM, Joanne Howl, DVM, Wayne Hunthausen, DVM, Meryl P. Littman, VMD, Deryl Troyer, DVM, and Beverly Adams. The author wishes to emphasize that any technical errors are her own.

All inquiries should be addressed to:
Barron's Educational Series, Inc.
250 Wireless Boulevard
Hauppauge, NY 11788
http://www.barronseduc.com

Library of Congress Catalog Card No. 98-46012
International Standard Book No. 0-7641-0753-4

Library of Congress Cataloging-in-Publication Data
Commings, Karen.
The manx : everything about purchase, care, nutrition, behavior, and training / Karen Commings ; illustrated by Michelle Earle-Bridges.
p.   cm. — (Complete pet owner's manual)
Includes bibliographical references (p.   ) and index.
ISBN 0-7641-0753-4
1. Manx cat. I. Title. II. Series.
SF449.M36C65   1999
636.8'22—dc21   98-46012
                                                      CIP

Printed in Hong Kong
9 8 7 6 5 4 3 2 1

Cats without tails exist here and there throughout the world, but the Manx is the only cat bred specifically to have no tail. Although the origin of the Manx is unknown, its lack of a tail is attributed to a mutation that occurred hundreds of years ago within the cat population on the Isle of Man, a dot of land in the Irish Sea, between England and Ireland. A prized show cat, the Manx is also a favorite household pet. Its intelligence and agreeable temperament make it easier to train than most breeds, and its playfulness and roly-poly appearance endear it to children as well as adults.